THIS
MYSTERIOUS
HUMAN NATURE

BY JAMES M. GILLIS, C.S.P.

So Near Is God

JAMES M. GILLIS

OF THE PAULIST FATHERS

THIS

MYSTERIOUS

HUMAN NATURE

CHARLES SCRIBNER'S SONS

New York

Nihil obstat

JOHN A. GOODWINE, J.C.D.
Censor Librorum

Imprimatur

✠ FRANCIS CARDINAL SPELLMAN
Archbishop of New York

The *nihil obstat* and *imprimatur* are official declarations that a book or pamphlet
is free of doctrinal or moral error. No implication is contained therein that those
who have granted the *nihil obstat* and *imprimatur* agree with the contents,
opinions or statements expressed.

DEDICATION

THIS little book is dedicated to Katherine Crofton for many years the "right-hand man" of the author in his editorial and other literary activities.

Such high intelligence, loyalty, good judgment and whole-souled dedication to a cause as that of Miss Crofton are to be met with, if at all, only once in a lifetime.

TABLE OF CONTENTS

V CHRISTIANITY: THE TOUCHSTONE
Essays in Practical Ethics

PART I

THIS MYSTERIOUS
HUMAN NATURE

Chapter 1

This Mysterious Human Nature

SOMEWHAT more than a half century ago Ernst Haeckel of Jena wrote a book titled *The Riddle of the Universe*. It was translated into all the principal languages, seized upon and taken for authentic by the millions who read "popular science," prefer it diluted and don't know or don't care if it is distorted. Haeckel was somewhat of a scientist, but much more a propagandist, a showman and to a degree a charlatan. He claimed that the riddle of the universe was at long last explained, its secret captured, brought to hand, dissected, analyzed, and the findings recorded and catalogued. Materialism, monism, atheism, was the answer to the riddle.

A generation later a scientist of a quite different stripe, Sir James Jeans, wrote two books, *The Universe Around Us,* and *The Mysterious Universe.* The latter was in effect a rejection of the dogmatism of some of his forebears in science, and a demonstration of the fact that the world in which we live and the myriad worlds that surround and as it were engulf our little world, remain after the last analysis a prodigious puzzle, unexplained and perhaps forever unexplainable, bewildering, incomprehensible and, as one might say, impossible and incredible.

Now that the secret has escaped again, the riddle is more puzzling than ever, the mystery is deeper and wider and no one dares any more to dogmatize. Only one thing is certain: the trend of the better scientific thought is away from materialism—science tends more and more to agree with religion that the

3

universe is infinitely mysterious. It seems to me, therefore, that the stage is now set for the entrance of a psychologist as capable in his line as Jeans or Eddington or Millikan or Einstein in theirs—a psychologist who shall demonstrate and illuminate the fact that not only the universe but man is mysterious; that the riddle of the human mind is more puzzling, the secret of the human heart more elusive, than the mystery of the inanimate universe. The riddle, enigma, the mystery *par excellence* is Man.

Not that the heart and mind and soul of man have remained unstudied; human nature has been scrutinized, probed, analyzed, a thousand times more intimately than the heavens or the earth or the elements. Before man developed any special interest in the stars above his head or the earth beneath his feet, or in what lay hidden hundreds of fathoms deep beneath the surface of the sea, he was immensely curious about himself; he was digging into his own heart, making desperate attempts to explain himself to himself. Poetry came into the world long before science; and poetry is largely an attempt to explore and to interpret the mystery of man. So too, drama and fiction which as it were take man out of himself, parade himself before his own eyes across a stage or through the pages of a book so that he may see himself; and philosophy which, as the first and greatest of human sages has said, is comprised in the phrase "Know Thyself!" Sometimes I incline to the suspicion that Socrates spoke that adage tongue in cheek. "Know Thyself!" As if any man could! Another genius in the difficult, delicate art of self-analysis, St. Augustine, added a note, "O God, make me know myself: make me know Thee." There is a catch even in that prayer. I can hardly know myself any more than I can know God. Only God can fully know man. Of Jesus Christ it is written, "He knew what was in man; He needed not that any man should tell Him," but Christ was God as well as man and it is in His capacity as God that He knows man. A biographer of Napoleon Bonaparte quotes his hero as saying, "All my life I have studied men. I know men." But the obvious fact is that Napoleon did not know men—or if he knew men he did not know man. If he had known man he would not have died beaten, disgraced, and in exile. Shakespeare—the myriad-minded Shakespeare—probably knew man better than any other poet or dramatist or philosopher. Certainly he made a life study of man; he tracked every emotion and mood and thought and passion of man to its secret lair in the human heart, dragged it out, incarnated it in man or woman, king, peasant, soldier, student, lover, clown, clothed it in ermine or fustian or in mourner's weeds, and made it "strut and fret its hour upon the stage." If ever a man revealed ourselves to ourselves, it was that all-but-omniscient Shakespeare. But even he was compelled in the end to confess that he couldn't solve the riddle of man. Witness the famous monologue, "What a piece of work is man!" continuing, "how like an angel!" but concluding, "this quintessence of dust!"

And there, as near as any man has hit upon it, is the solution of the riddle; the "angel," the "paragon," "infinite in reason," "in form and moving express and admirable," is also dust and quintessence of dust! Man is a mystery because he is a bundle of contradictions. "Richard Yea and Nay" was one of the nicknames of Coeur de Lion. But every man is Yea and Nay. Angel and beast, sublime, debased, pure spirit tangled in obscene flesh, courageous and cowardly, wise, stupid, gross, groveling, sordid, earthy; noble, high-minded, afire with spiritual ambition, angelic, more than angelic—"Have I not said ye are Gods?"—a clod and a star; a worm and a lion. Lion? say also hyena, jackal; the stuff of which heroes are made and dung under the feet; cruel and kind; builder of hospitals and of torture chambers, good Samaritan and grand inquisitor, giving his life for his friend, yes even for his enemy, but selfish as Satan; loyal as Peter or Paul, treacherous as Judas; quick to take fire and rush into battle to right any wrong, real or imagined; but sluggish, lethargic, tolerant of long-standing corruption, shrugging the shoulders or even winking at injustice; impetuous enthusiast, and bloodless stoic;

a furious fighter when caught in "the fell clutch of circumstance," and yet "serene, indifferent to fate"; generous, chivalrous, Quixotic, idealistic, sordid, mercenary, materialistic. Angel and beast did I say? Angel and devil! the devils were angels. Man is a child of God, heir to the kingdom of heaven, but a rebel against God; having indeed a home and a Father in heaven but preferring the fleshpots of earth; self-exiled, sitting on the dung heap, consorting with swine, too dispirited to arise and go to his Father; but again leaping up, donning the armor of God, battling his way through legions of devils, storming the ramparts of the skies, thundering at the gates, taking the kingdom of heaven by storm, shouting the tremendous challenge, "Lift up your gates, O ye princes, and be ye lifted up, ye everlasting portals," as if to say, "O God, command that the gate be opened, or I will break it down." And that is the man, the very same man who puts his head in his hands and cries, "God be merciful to me, a sinner; I am weak and in labors from my youth, my enemies are camped about me and they are stronger than I."

Curious, mad, incredible contradiction, man! an utterly insoluble riddle; unbelievable impossible combination of hero and coward, beast and devil and God! Some one attempting to define God (God of course cannot be defined) called Him "the hidden synthesis of irreconcilables." There is a hint of truth in that, though it is, as it stands, theologically inaccurate, but though it is not true of God, it does seem to be true of man; he is indeed a synthesis of irreconcilables. In him the flesh and the spirit are at war, and not only flesh and spirit, but devils and angels. What wonder that the gentle à Kempis, after saying, "*this* shall puzzle thee," and "*that* shall puzzle thee," adds, "but most of all thou shalt often be a puzzle to thyself." What wonder, too, if the poets, though they penetrate flesh and blood and see into the heart, confess in the end that they cannot fathom man, and that the dramatists who take the world but as the world—a stage where every man must play a part—observe man as he makes his exit and his entrance, watch him strut his brief hour, as the curtain rings down, leave us with the despondent reflection, "Life is a tale told by an idiot full of sound and fury signifying nothing."

Shakespeare gave it up. Dante gnashed his teeth at it all. Italy with its feuds and internecine battles, its conflicts between Guelphs and Ghibellines, was a symbol of the conflict of savagery with civilization, heaven and hell, God and Satan, in every human heart. Shakespeare and Dante? Even David, the divinely inspired prophet was bewildered. "What is man?" cries he, and under inspiration answers himself: "Man is a little lower than the angels. Thou hast set him over all the works of Thy hands." But in the same book, almost the same psalm, he confesses ruefully, "Man when he was in honor did not understand; he is compared to senseless beasts, and is become like to them. This way of theirs is a stumbling block to them . . . They are laid in hell like sheep; death shall feed upon them."

There in a word is the heart of the paradox, the center and core of the anomaly of man. Heaven and hell are in the heart. God and Satan are tearing at each other. The Easter Hymn has it: *Mors et vita duello conflixere mirando*. Life and death are at grips in horrendous conflict. The heart and soul of man is a battleground of Titans, supernatural Titans. And what is worse— if anything can be worse than the conflict of God and Satan—is that man is at odds with himself as to which side he shall take. Sometimes loyal, he stands with God; sometimes treacherous he finds himself fighting or following the fight on the side of Satan. Alternately, or even simultaneously, he is good and bad, saint, sinner, animal, angel, hero, coward, slave, soldier, victim and victor, winning, losing, pathetic, tragic, but in the end let us hope, triumphant—this is man!

Chapter 2

Children of God, and Rebels!

OPPONENTS of the Christian religion are endlessly ingenious in discovering or inventing objections against our faith and our system of worship. One of their most plausible criticisms is that we undervalue human nature. We call ourselves "miserable sinners," we bow our head in shame and repentence. We cry "Lord have mercy!" We strike our breast making the triple invocation "Lord, I am not worthy!" We bend the knee before we even venture into a pew in the church; when we say our prayers, we assume the attitude of a supplicant; on occasion we prostrate ourselves wholly, all but touching the ground with our forehead; we observe penitential seasons during which we repeatedly chant the *Miserere*, "Have Mercy!" and the *De Profundis*, "Out of the Depths!" Once a year for three successive nights we perform a solemn ceremony built upon the Lamentations of Jeremias sung to a rhythm more poignant than that to be heard at the Wailing Wall of Jerusalem.

All this, we are told, is unworthy of human dignity, and subtly demoralizing. "Get up off your knees," they tell us. "Lift your forehead from the dust. Shake the ashes off your head. Stand erect. Look the world in the eye. Tell yourself you're as good as any man and better than most. Yes, look your *God* in the face. Deal with Him on a basis of equality. Stop cringing, stop wailing. Rid yourself of the sense of inferiority."

Our reply to that formidable indictment is that our human nature is a mass of contradictions and our conduct, following

8

our nature, must therefore be paradoxical. Those who launch these objections and accusations against our belief and our practice have fallen into the "either-or" fallacy. They think we must *either* do this *or* do that; the truth is we must *both* do this *and* do that. They cannot understand that in virtue of our divided nature, sometimes we must bury our face in the dust and at other times look our God in the eye: one moment at the Communion rail we strike our breast and cry, "Lord, I am not worthy," but the very next instant we pray, "Lord, come into my heart and make me one with Thee." On certain days at certain services we chant *Miserere* but on another day we shout *Alleluia*. Unreasonable? Contradictory? Not to those who understand the complexity of human nature, the conflict in the heart of man. Only to those who think of man as all one sort of thing and nothing of another sort, all angel and no animal, or all animal and no angel, will our faith or our practice seem bewildering.

Truly the Christian religion is a tissue of paradoxes. And the greatest paradox of all, if I may say so with infinite reverence, is Christ Himself. "I am a worm and no man," said He, and yet with a whip of cords and with the more stinging lash of His wrath He drove the money-changers from the temple. "Turn the other cheek," said He, but when the servant of the high priest smote Him on the face, He said with superb self-possession, "If I have spoken evil, give testimony of the evil; but if good, why smitest thou Me?" "He was led like a lamb to the slaughter, not opening His mouth," but His silence made King Herod squirm upon his throne, and put Pontius Pilate at a disadvantage. When Pilate finally persuaded Jesus to speak, by the device of putting Him under oath: "I adjure Thee by the Living God that Thou tell us if Thou be the Son of God," our Savior replied with simple dignity, "Thou sayest it." When the governor, attempted to start an argument—imagine the Roman potentate offering to argue with the Galilean peasant—"Dost Thou not know that I have power to crucify Thee and power to let Thee go," Jesus made the definitive reply, "Thou shouldst have no power if it were not given thee by God."

There can be no doubt as to Who was the Master in that brief exchange: the Pale Galilean already had conquered. He had overpowered Pilate with a word as He had withered Herod with a glance. If Pilate and Herod are in hell, I imagine the essence of their agony must be in the look of the eyes of Jesus, burning eternally into their souls. And yet it was only the look of a lamb.

As with Christ, so with all true Christians. When St. Barbara the Roman Virgin was taken to a lupanar to be corrupted before being tortured and killed, the mistress of that place of shame reported to the judge: "We can do nothing with her. You might as well command these stone walls to flow like water as to change the resolution of that obstinate girl." The martyrs, led into the arena, kissed the hands of their jailers and executioners, but when called upon in the presence of some scores of thousands of spectators to put a pinch of incense in the burning brazier before the statue of Jupiter or Venus or the Emperor, they laughed in the face of the judge and spat upon the idols. The omnipotence of Rome meant nothing to them; they were not overawed; the howling of the mob could not intimidate them. They had indeed burrowed underground into the Catacombs. They were in consequence despised as *gens lucifuga,* a people that fled the light. Dragged out like rats or moles blinking into the sunlight, they did indeed seem an ignoble and despicable lot, the proper butt for the contempt of the mob; but once in the arena, faced with instruments of torture or with wild beasts, they took on instinctively a dignity like that of their Master Who had so quietly and so surely manifested His superiority over Herod and Pilate.

So is it with all the lesser martyrs who have inherited something of the serene fortitude of Jesus and His immediate followers. If a man is a true Christian, he is an aristocrat and a king even though he is held as a slave or reputed a criminal. You may grind his face into the earth, ply the lash upon his shoulders until he lies prostrate in a pool of his own blood, you may put the gyves upon his wrists and ankles and rivet him with a chain to a rock in the depths of a dungeon. But he will pray and sing and make merry in his heart; he will recreate his spirit with visions of paradise, enjoy ineffable colloquy with God; he will speak with God and God will speak with him. Those who have read and absorbed the truest of all romances, the most thrilling of all dramas—the lives of the saints—will know that I am not now permitting myself a rhetorical fling. I am narrating badly and without imagination a fact that has been verified a hundred thousand times and more in our history—the paradoxical fact that the meek and humble Christian who seems so contemptible in the eyes of the proud, and who indeed confesses before God and man that he *is* contemptible, nonetheless possesses in the unsounded depths of his soul something of the superb dignity of the poor Palestinian carpenter's Son who destroyed King Herod's assurance with a look and demoralized Pontius Pilate with a word.

The Christian doctrine of the freedom of man's will fortified by Divine Grace leads us even further. With no desire to be melodramatic, indeed with the conscious purpose of avoiding oratory, I say with all soberness that our religion teaches us to look not only man but the devil in the eye. We bend the knee, but not to man; we cringe and cower in the dust but not before Satan. We kneel to God, we prostrate ourselves before God, we cry our lamentations and our *misereres* into His ears but we are not awed by men or by devils. In the presence of pompous self-important powerful men we only laugh—poor puppets strutting their short hour clothed with the rags of a little brief authority. As for the evil one—before him we take on a supernatural confidence. We believe that he has power, but we know that against him we have greater power, even the omnipotence of God. We remember that when Satan took Our Lord up to the pinnacle of the temple to tempt Him, all he could say in the end was, "Cast Thyself down!" And we have caught the truth behind that symbol. Satan cannot cast any man down. Only man himself can damn himself. At the last moment of even the most violent temptation, the spirit of evil must stand aside and say, "Do it yourself. Damn your own soul. I cannot cast you down." Even Satan has his limitations. We know that. We recognize that we are independent even of the prince of evil. He cannot put us in hell, but we can send him back to hell.

The freedom wherewith God our Creator has endowed us carries us far. But we must not shrink from the last conclusion. God has made us independent even of Himself. He could coerce us, but He has declared that He never will. So, it is possible for man to defy not only man, not only Satan, but God. Man may stand in the face of God and cry, *"Non Serviam"*: "I will not serve Thee!" Just as a nation may put a weapon in the hands of the citizen, expecting him to fight in the defense of his country, and the citizen may turn rebel and use the weapon against his country; so it is possible that the creature may use the endowments of God to dishonor God. This freedom is a wonderful gift, a divine prerogative, but it remains a perilous privilege. Even so, God has evidently thought it better that we should have it than not have it. There is a risk in bestowing upon man something that makes him like God. But God, Who wished us to be His children and therefore made us to His Own image and likeness, takes the chance, so to speak, of our turning rebels and traitors against Him.

This too, like all the other contradictions in our nature, makes life interesting, dramatic, fateful. But every true man, trusted with a great responsibility will rise to great heights. *Noblesse Oblige.* Since God has trusted us, shall we not assure Him with all earnestness that His trust is not misplaced and that He will not rue the decision to create us free? We shall be sons of God and not rebels.

PART II

ST. AUGUSTINE
AND HIS
CONFESSIONS

Chapter 3

Seeking Truth and Finding God

OVER a period of fifteen hundred years the *Confessions of St. Augustine* has been read by uncounted millions of people in every civilized Christian land. But not every one who reads it has the insight to detect that its plot, so to speak, is triple. First, most obviously, it tells the story of the struggle of a passionate man to break the bonds of fleshly enjoyment, to be free with the freedom of the spirit. Along with the story of that titanic battle runs the story of his indefatigable search for truth. Gradually it becomes evident to the author and to the reader that Augustine's search for truth was really the pursuit of God.

The first phase of his triple conflict was the battle against carnal lust. Charles Bigg of Christ Church, Oxford, one of the best of a half-hundred translators of the precious classic, says in a wise and eloquent Introduction: "Augustine went down into the very depths and came face to face with the dragon that dwells there, with the facts of the sensual nature in their barbarous simplicity. There are some who appear never to have had this experience, and they find it possible, to their own great loss, to view religion merely as the most interesting of speculative problems. But Augustine could not take this cool scientific view. He was in the torrent, not watching it from the shore. He was an intensely human man, strongly sensuous and keenly intelligent. The whole of his nature was at war. Reason could not control, desire would not obey, and there could be no peace except in submission to a higher law, which should embrace and harmonize both antagonists."

Does some one exclaim: "Harmonize the antagonists! harmonize reason and passion! Must not reason destroy passion, or at least paralyze passion? How can there be harmony between such fiercely powerful antithetical forces as those of flesh and spirit?" The answer is that Augustine was a supreme psychologist and a great moralist. The proper word is harmony, not destruction. Nature is not to be obliterated. Flesh and spirit are to be coordinated. The perfect man is one in whom, as the *Following of Christ* says, "Passion is subject to reason and reason subject to God." Puritans in all ages have made the tragic blunder of thinking the human body ignoble, shameful, a creation of the devil. But in Catholic theology the body, no less than the soul, is a creature of God. No creature of God is to be held abominable or to be destroyed. Virtue consists in the right ordering of all creatures of God: passion subject to reason; reason subject to God.

Augustine was clear-sighted enough to see that the flesh is of itself good. If it leads a man into filth and shame it is at the prompting of the mind and the will. At the very threshold of his famous and ever memorable description of his struggle with himself in the garden of Alypius at Cassicium, one of the most dramatic and fascinating passages in all literature, Augustine stops to puzzle over what he calls a strange anomaly. "Whence is it," he says, "and why?" . . . Mind commands body and there is instant obedience; mind commands mind and there is rebellion." Evidently he understands that the battle is not between body and soul. The emotions and passions, the uprisings and rebellions of the flesh occur at the command or with the connivance of the spirit. If the flesh at times acts automatically without the knowledge and consent of the spirit, its action is neither good nor bad. What makes it good or bad is the dictation of the will. It does not suffice, therefore, that will should command flesh; will must command will if the flesh is to obey. And, says St. Augustine, "The debate raged in my heart, myself battling against myself." If against this analysis of carnal temptation the text be alleged from St. Paul, "The flesh lusteth against the spirit: and the spirit against the flesh, for these are contrary one to another," it need only be remarked that the word "flesh" in that passage does not mean the body but an evil will. Amongst the works of the flesh, the Apostle enumerates "enmities, contentions, emulations, wraths, quarrels" and other sins that are obviously not of the body but of the mind and will.

The long bitter struggle undergone by the hot-blooded North African youth, with the fire of Latin and perhaps Phoenician ancestors in his blood, before he achieved command and control of carnal passion, is recorded with no less dramatic power than that of Shakespeare or Sophocles in a marvelous masterpiece within a masterpiece—the Ninth Book of the *Confessions*. But, after all, that part of his battle was the least important. The struggle for truth gave him more anguish than the struggle for purity. Not that he finished one battle before he took up the other. The two were concurrent. Struggles, like troubles, seldom come singly. As we guard the citadel against besiegers from without, we have to turn and deal with rebellion on the part of those within. Of old on the field of battle a particularly gallant knight would fight not with one sword but with two.

So with Augustine. The battle for purity would have been stiff enough if he had not at the same time to battle for truth. Those of us who possess the truth are aware of that. If we have one rebellion on our hands we would not welcome another. When the flesh is seething, the blood boiling, it would be multiplied anguish if the mind were to revolt, if, while we fight for virtue, some devil in the brain should mock us with questions: "What is virtue? What is vice? You fool, nothing is either good or bad, right or wrong." As a matter of fact, that is precisely what does happen, as many a man knows who has to put up a stiff struggle to master his passions while his convictions seem to run out on him.

In Augustine's case the tempter came in the form of Manicheeism. Here is this young man, disgusted with his vices, fighting them courageously if not quite confidently, when there appear the disciples of Faustus, leader of the Oriental sect of Manichees. They tell Augustine that neither he nor any man is responsible for his evil deeds, that the sense of guilt in his conscience is only an illusion. In that immoral dictum we recognize the ages-old doctrine, flattering and meant to be soothing, which tells a man struggling and agonizing with temptation that there is really no such thing as moral responsibility; that we do what we do because we cannot help doing it; and that since we cannot help doing it we need not and should not castigate our own conscience.

The Manichees claimed to have a magic cure for all such infirmities. Nothing is really wrong with you, they explained, but —illogically enough—they added, "Come to us and we will set you right." Augustine, it must be admitted, fell captive to their wiles, but not for long. There never was in all the history of thought a quicker, keener, more penetrating mind than his. One of the great sentences in the *Confessions* is the one in which he says he was commencing to disentangle the reality of things from the trickery of words.

May we hesitate for one moment to remark that here is one of the sentences, scattered with prodigal hand throughout the *Confessions,* that makes us love the little book? The reality of things tangled in the trickery of words! The wise man is the man who knows how to unravel the tangled skein of words and release the real thing, the fact, the truth. A great many people ostensibly educated, even learned, go through life from beginning to end without knowing a thing from a word, a fact from a fallacy, a slogan from a truth. Augustine's was not one of those dulled intellects. His was a creative mind. A mind must be critical before it can be creative. It must clear away the ruins of error before it can build the truth. Some there are who live and die and never learn to think because their brains are cluttered up with intellectual debris. There is no clear path through their mind on which they can make progress. They are lost as if in the twisted and tangled undergrowth of a tropical jungle. There is no more chance of their getting free than there is of the sculptured Laocoön shaking off the serpents that wind around his arms and his legs and his torso.

Pardon the interlude. Perhaps it is not all interlude. If St. Augustine had not learned to extricate the reality of things from the entanglement of words, he never would have found the truth.

In our own day there is many a professor, lecturer, pedagogue occupying what is usually entitled grandiloquently a "chair of learning" at some wealthy powerful overgrown university who fascinates, hypnotizes, deludes the young folks who sit under him. In Augustine's day the professor of Manicheeism (it seems strange now to speak of Manicheeism as a rival of Christianity as it will seem odd a thousand years hence to recall a half-dozen now prevalent philosophies that lure the young away from the Gospel), I say the professor *par excellence* of this system of pretentious pseudo-wisdom and pseudo-science was one named Faustus. "Wait till Faustus comes," said the lesser lights of Manicheeism, when the young Augustine had torn away their intellectual disguise and made them appear ridiculous. "Wait for Faustus." When Faustus came, says Augustine: "I found him a man of charming manner and pleasant address, who said just what the others used to say but in much more agreeable style. The butler was most elegant, and the goblet was more costly, but my thirst remained. Already my ears had been satiated with such things; and now they did not seem any better, because they were better said, nor true because dressed up in rhetoric, nor could I think the man's soul wise, because he looked wise and his speech was pleasing . . . Already I had learned that nothing ought to seem true because it is well expressed, nor false because the word-symbols are inelegant; yet again, that nothing is true because rudely delivered, nor false because the diction is brilliant; but that wisdom and folly are like meats that are wholesome or unwholesome, and that either kind of meat can be served up in silver or in delf, that is to say in courtly or in homely phrase."

As long as Faustus remained on the platform and Augustine was unable to engage him in intimate conversation, he managed to appear learned. But when the eager young African finally made his way through the crowd of sycophantic adherents of the professor, he was disillusioned. The pain of disillusionment was softened a trifle because Faustus seems to have been a likable person. He was modest. "He knew that he did not know and was not ashamed to confess his ignorance," says Augustine. What he says further about the deflated sage of the Manichees is interesting and edifying as a light on Augustine's own charitable mind. "He was not absolutely ignorant of his ignorance, and he did not choose to be entangled by hasty assertions in a position where there was no way out or back; and for this I liked him all the better. For the modesty of candor is more beautiful than the problems which I desired to solve; and this I found to be his temper in all difficult and abstruse matters."

Nonetheless the searcher for truth was baffled. He despaired of other doctors. But though disillusioned he was not discouraged. He thanks God that his discovery of the ignorance of a philosopher turned out to be a step along the way to the discovery of the wisdom of Christ.

For one thing he never lost his deeply seated confidence, that truth *can* be discovered. He could never have taken the intellectually suicidal position of many of the moderns who maintain that truth is forever elusive; that though we seek truth we shall never find it. How it can be that persons who profess agnosticism still study philosophy remains a riddle to any logical mind. Aristotle said that man is born to know, and naturally is led to seek to know even more and more. A modern philosopher, who indeed modestly concealed his philosophical acumen behind the pretense of being only a journalist, G. K. Chesterton, said: "The human mind is an instrument made for the purpose of discovering truth. If it fails to discover truth there must be something wrong with the instrument." In the canticle of Isaias we read in one verse "Verily Thou art a hidden God, the God of Israel," but almost immediately the Lord answered the prophet's complaint, "I have not spoken in secret, in a dark place . . . I have not said . . . Seek Me in vain." God is truth. If God is not hidden, altogether undiscoverable, neither is truth undiscoverable. When Pontius Pilate asked the question of Jesus, "What is Truth?" the answer might have been "Stretch out your hand, Pilate, and you shall touch Truth."

But agnostics, modern and ancient, have no passion for truth. They are easily discouraged. Some one wrote an article years ago on "Cowardly Agnosticism." It might have been Craven Agnosticism. Disconsolate Agnosticism. Too quickly and too easily disconsolate. Truth can be found if you seek it. You shall not miss it if you love it. But you must love truth passionately. You must seek it with the unflagging persistence of an explorer bent upon the discovery of a new continent, not to be frightened, not to be tempted to give up or to turn back because of unruly elements or still more unruly men. A good example of an agnostic might be a navigator, an explorer in midocean, who with hope long deferred, provisions running low, a muttering rebellious, all but mutinous crew, would say, "Sailors, I give up. I had hoped and believed that there was land ahead. Now, of course, I admit that there isn't. Or if there is, no man can find it."

Columbus was no such coward. He came to know and his disheartened crew came to know there *was* land. There is always land. You cannot sail the seas without discovering land, if you sail long enough with sufficient courage and patience, and above all with a fierce determination to find what you seek.

As of land, so of undiscovered truth. There is always truth. Sail the seas of knowledge and you shall come upon truth. But you must sail on and on and not turn back. You must not falter or be frightened. You must not be dissuaded by a cowardly crew, a cowardly crew even of philosophers, of agnostic philosophers, who are after all, in the realm of knowledge, what in any other realm we should call defeatists.

Augustine was a Columbus, sailing the intellectual seas in search of truth. Once he had started he would not turn back. Disillusionment was his, time and again. One system after another he tried and found to be a mental mirage. On he went in spite of turbulent storms, mental and moral storms, in comparison with which the riot of the elements in midocean is inconsiderable.

He had his reward. He arrived. Like the valiant discoverer who hoped to find only a backdoor to an old continent but found instead the front door to a new continent, this discoverer who went in search of Truth found God. From time to time as he progressed he caught glimpses of the fact that God is Truth, and that if only he could lay hands on Truth he would possess God. That was indeed the spur, the goad that would not let him rest. If truth were only truth, something to be found at the end of a treasure hunt, something of no value that might be thrown away as soon as found, he would have had no incentive. But he came rather early in the search to realize that Truth is God. So he was enraptured with the prospect of catching up with truth, and when he found it he burst forth in continual canticles of thanksgiving and praise. As he says, he "babbled like a child." But those childish babblings, as it happens, are the babblings of one who was a great philosopher and a poet. Those "babblings" are a part of the world's greatest literature.

There was a time in the beginning, and for perhaps a year after his beginning when he had to say that he loved error and cleaved to it, hated to lose error because losing error he feared to lose delight. But when once his mind and heart had been ravished with a glimpse of truth as God, he was determined to be done with error and to capture God. He says, "Where I found Truth, there I found God."

And that I would say to those who are in anguish because they have found neither Truth nor God, that is the goad that should prod them on. Seek and ye shall find. And if the intellectual search be impeded by moral obstacles, seek and fight. You shall find at one and the same moment the Good and the Beautiful as well as the True. And you shall know in that day that the Good and the True and the Beautiful are God.

Chapter 4

"Thou Hast Made Us For Thyself"

IT SOMETIMES happens that a man of prodigious genius who has written voluminously and has spoken even more than he has written, is remembered by the world at large as the author of one adage, one brief axiom.

The most profound and comprehensive intellect of the last fifteen hundred years was that of St. Augustine. At least such is my conviction. *My* conviction? The phrase smacks of arrogance. It is not merely *my* conviction. I share it with the whole world of learning. I have not merely borrowed it but have made it my own just as truly as if I alone had discovered it. All the world knows St. Augustine. He ranks with Socrates, Plato and Aristotle. Indeed, he outranks Socrates, as he does all other thinkers except, perhaps, St. Paul.

Not to elaborate the point, suffice it to say in the words of a great scholar who was particularly at home in the field of early Christian literature and patristic theology (Adolf Harnack), the whole Christian world has been thinking the thoughts and repeating the words of St. Augustine since his death early in the second quarter of the fifth century.

He wrote a whole library himself, and a library a hundred times larger has been written about him. With all that wealth of philosophic thought, the general populace is unacquainted, just as those who have heard or read of a great diamond—say the Kohinoor—or have seen it among the crown jewels of

England in the Tower of London do not know or care to know from what mine it came.

Even in their prayers devout Catholics and non-Catholics use words and phrases of St. Augustine, though they may never have heard of him, just as the man in the street quotes Shakespeare and the Bible without perhaps having read either Shakespeare or the Bible without knowing the origin of the phrases that form his mind and fall from his lips.

So much by way of introduction to the axiom chosen for comment in this chapter. "Thou has made us for Thyself, O God, and our hearts are restless until they find rest in Thee."

All religion is in that sentence; all philosophy, all the history of man, all the beauty and tragedy and pathos of human life. He who learns the wisdom so compactly pressed into that precious nugget is fortunate. He who does not learn it will go to his grave without even knowing why he was sent into the world or what he was aiming at. In a review of a book of poems I came upon a couple of sentences that made me stop and think and read once more—a rather rare experience from a book review. "There runs through these poems," said the critic, "the cry of despair, and emotional nostalgia which is fundamentally the cry of rootlessness. We have heard it before, in spiritual bitterness of the exile, the man isolate within himself." That particular poet found at last the cure for his nostalgia in religion—the Catholic religion. But there is a world of homesick persons rootless and restless who find neither cure nor solace. They are a lost battalion who know not how they came to be where they are, or how to return to the place whence they came. They are of that "lost generation" of which we hear so much, who have been torn by the roots from the world they knew and who cannot be transplanted in the world into which they have been flung.

They are like one who flounders around aimlessly in adolescence, arrives at young manhood, passes through it into middle age, and in some instances beyond middle age, but of whom we

have to say, "He never found himself." There is no more pathetic
figure than such a one. His is a real tragedy, much more so than
that of Hamlet, who indeed is at loose ends when we meet him in
the first scenes of the great play, and who vacillates a great deal,
but finally discovers something that he can do about the situation
and does it. But the member of the lost generation enters upon
the stage of life, wanders around bewildered, and goes off stage
without so much as knowing what the play is about, how he came
to be in it, what he should say or do, or even how he can make
a graceful exit.

Now, it is the mind of St. Augustine that if one has lost himself it is because he has lost God, or has never found God. But
unlike the man who has lost his way, or his battalion or his
generation or his homeland, the man who has lost himself doesn't
know what he has lost. His restlessness comes not from seeking
himself but from his not knowing what it is that he is seeking. Of
all baffling experiences this is the most torturesome—to be looking
for something we know not what. We have read of dungeons
with cells in which the prisoner can neither sit nor stand nor lie
down. He can only squirm, incessantly seeking for some position
of the body that will not be too great a torture. But there is a
spiritual dungeon too in which the mind and soul find no rest.
"Woe to the rash soul," says St. Augustine, "which hopes by
forsaking Thee, O God, to find something better. It tosses and
turns upon back and side and belly, but the bed is hard and
Thou alone art rest." He speaks of the soul that has forsaken
God. But if there is greater anguish, it is for the soul that has
never known God and is seeking Him. "I fled Him down the
nights and down the days," says the great poet Francis Thompson, "I fled Him down the arches of the years. I fled Him down
the labyrinthine ways of my own mind." There is doubtless
anguish for the man who runs away from God, knowing that he
cannot escape. But a soul that has never found God, and has
never known Him might say, "I *sought* Him down the arches

of the years: I sought Him down the labyrinthine ways of my own mind." And there is, I believe, sharper pain in seeking for God than in attempting to elude Him. The renegade from God is at least aware that he cannot outrun those "feet that follow after with unhurrying chase, and unperturbed pace, deliberate speed, majestic instancy." He cannot but know—and the poet continues—that God's "voice is round [him] like a bursting sea," and that the Being of God will surround him, close in on him, engulf him.

But the one who has not God, knows not God, never was near to God and so never ran from God, seeks here and there, high and low for what will fill the bottomless gap in his mind and soul. He may seek knowledge, like Faust, and finding no satisfaction in natural learning, sell his soul to the devil in return for the preternatural knowledge which it is not good for man to have. Like Faust, he will shrink with horror from the knowledge of the inscrutable mystery which the art of Mephistopheles unveils for him. He will then seek joy in physical passion and the release of emotion. Alternately he will shun his fellowmen and then plunge into the society of the mob, rubbing elbows with them, in the hope that some of the crude delight they obtain in their loutish pleasures may be communicated to him. But, as all thinking men know, man finds only disillusion and disgust in the flesh. He bargains with the devil not for a lifetime of happiness but for just one moment of perfect contentment.

That classic of literature, *Faust,* is unlike the *Confessions of St. Augustine,* which antedated it by fourteen hundred years, but the theme is the same. In fact it is the theme of every classic in all literature—the restless heart of man seeking joy where joy is not to be found. "Oh ye children of men," cries out St. Augustine, "why will ye still still tread those steep and stony paths? Ye are seeking for rest where no rest is to be found. Seek what ye seek but it is not where ye seek it. We are seeking a happy life in the land of death; it is not there."

Augustine knew. He had gone through the mill. Unlike the usual voluptuary who knows only the joys of the flesh and is a stranger to those of the intellect, Augustine had gone deep into all sorts of substitutes for Divine Joy, and they had failed him.

It is a commonplace of human wisdom that animal pleasure cannot satisfy man since man is no mere animal. But perhaps it is not so well realized that not even the delights of the mind are sufficient for us. "Is a man pleasing to Thee, O Lord God of Truth," asks St. Augustine, "because he knows these things?"— that is to say, who knows the things the learned know? "Nay, unhappy is the man who knows these things and knows not Thee. Happy is the man who knows Thee even if he knows not these things."

This feature of the *Confessions* of St. Augustine has, I think, been obscured or neglected. Every one knows that St. Augustine sinned grievously in the flesh. And almost everybody takes his *Confessions* to be the story of how he broke away from carnal delights and found comfort in the purer pleasures of the mind. He does indeed confess that he "plunged headlong into love." "I was beloved," he says, "I attained my wish, the bondage of clandestine fruition." But he thanks God Who "embittered that cup of sweetness." He found that in seeking what is called love, he had "riveted around himself the chain of woe." "I was scourged," he says, "with red-hot iron rods." When he came to himself or rather when he came to God; when he had broken those chains and burst those bonds, he found that "it was joy to cast away what he had feared to lose." "My soul," he says, "was delivered from gnawing anxieties . . . from wallowing in the mud and scratching the swinish itch of lust." In his joy he "prattled like a child to God."

But the delivery of his soul from the ignominy and the anguish of carnal passion is not the only theme of the *Confessions*. What Augustine aims to convey to his fellow men is that neither the joys of flesh nor of spirit, neither lust and debauchery on the one hand, nor philosophy and the fine arts on the other, can assuage the thirst of the soul. Plato speaks of that "dear delight philosophy." Augustine knew that delight from his youth. He had experienced the ecstasy of intellectual pursuits; as a creative thinker, he had time and again felt the thrill of a new discovery in the world of the mind. But his theme is not the superiority of mental pleasures over fleshly delights. The *Confessions,* that incomparable little masterpiece of psychology and religion, is really a demonstration of the fact that neither the carnal nor the intellectual can satisfy man. Man, we say, is more than a beast. But man is also more than a mind. There is that in us which likens us to God and since we are like to God, nothing really contents us but the kind of joy that God has in Himself. There is nothing in flesh or in spirit, nothing in art or in life, nothing in heaven or earth that can give us perfect and lasting contentment. Only God is great enough to satisfy the soul. He has made us for Himself and our hearts are restless until they find rest in Him.

Man lifts up his voice to God and cries: "O God, when I had no being at all Thou didst create me; and for the boon of life I thank Thee. Together with life Thou hast bestowed upon me faculties of intelligence and free will, Thou hast given me power to know; to know the world about me, to know myself, to know Thee. For the Godlike power of knowing, I thank Thee. For the dangerous but precious gift of free will, which makes me under Thee lord of the world, master of creation, dictator of my own destiny, I thank Thee. Beyond and above these natural blessings Thou hast endowed my soul with supernatural graces, with faith, and the power to pray, yes even with the amazing privilege of loving Thee. In this most of all hast Thou shown Thine mercy that Thou hast permitted me to love Thee.

"But, O my God, I remain still unsatisfied. Thou mayest ransack all Thy heavenly kingdom, gather together all gifts and graces and drop them into my heart. But they cannot fill that insatiable heart of mine. Thou hast made me man, but Thou hast given me the capacity of a God. Nothing on earth or in heaven satisfies me unless Thou bestow upon me Thyself. My heart remains empty unless Thou fill it with Thyself."

We must not imagine that such a prayer can come only from the lips of a saint and a mystic. All mankind makes that prayer. Not indeed in just those words but with "unsearchable groanings." We often pray for some one thing or other and we think we know what we want. But what we really desire—whether we recognize it or not and no matter in what words we frame our wishes—what we really desire is nothing less than God. If we pray for a spiritual or a temporal favor, it is only a pretext or a disguise. We don't really want that favor. Deep down in our hearts we are saying, "O God, I want not Thy gifts; I want Thee." If we obtain God's gifts and not God, we remain spiritually hungry as before.

Here then for those who can read it, is the lesson of the *Confessions* of St. Augustine. Like the psalmist, he hungers and thirsts for the living God. His battle is not for virtue or knowledge, but for God. As with Augustine, so with all of us. We may not have his gift of self-scrutiny. We do not know ourselves as well as he. We are not all endowed with intellectual and spiritual genius. But in our hearts we feel what he felt. To us as to the saint, all the treasures of heaven and earth are as nothing, until we lay hold on God. Unless we have God we have not anything. When we have Him, we have all. Nothing short of the All contents us. We come first and last, again and again to the same conviction: "Thou hast made us for Thyself, O God, and our hearts are restless until they rest in Thee."

Chapter 5

"Myself Battling Myself"

"The life of man upon earth is a warfare," says the patriarch Job. A triple warfare, we usually say, against the world, the flesh, and the devil. Not merely triple but multiple, against not three, but a thousand enemies—environment; evil inheritance; customs, traditions, maxims of worldly wisdom, false philosophies, systems of ethics that condescend to human infirmity and compromise with prevalent wickedness; bad example even from those in high position; public vice, organized and impudent; indecent entertainment, theatrical and other; skepticism in the matter of religion; cynicism about corruption in public and private life; fatalism, ancient and Oriental but with pseudo-scientific modification to fit it for the western world, a fatalism or defeatism which holds that man is not a free responsible agent, that sin is an illusion or, if real, unavoidable.

But the catalogue of dangers that surround and beat upon the godly man is interminable. He who would keep himself "unspotted from the world" as St. James says, will find himself in a kind of battle royal, in the ring with many adversaries, who attack him from one side or another, behind or before, or all together with no sense of sportsmanship, no rules and no restrictions.

If a man falls ill and takes to his bed with some ailment or other, he becomes a mark for a dozen diseases. They seem always to be hovering about in the atmosphere waiting to pounce upon him when he is down. Troubles never come singly. Neither, it would sometimes seem, do sicknesses. Or dangers. Or enemies. There is truth in the ancient myths about the giant who, being thrown to the ground, sprang up always stronger, and of the dragon which being slashed to pieces became so many new dragons. Truly, therefore, the life of man upon earth is a warfare, a general war against a multitude of enemies.

But what I have in mind for consideration in this chapter is not man's battle with his earthly environment, or for that matter, with his unearthly adversary, Satan, but with himself. Or, as St. Augustine puts it, "myself battling myself." We sometimes say of a man that "he is his own worst enemy." Such a man is neither unique nor unusual. He is no rarity or oddity. He is the universal man. He is Everyman. Or again we say of a man that "he seems to be at odds with himself." But who is there that is not at odds with himself? Aren't we all? If there be on this earth a man who has achieved perfect equilibrium, absolute mental and emotional balance, I wonder if such a one can still be called "human." Perfect quiescence of the mind and of the passions would seem to indicate that one had entered upon a sort of Nirvana.

Whether such a condition is possible here below may be debatable. But the question may also arise as to whether it is desirable. When a patient, stricken with a possibly fatal disease, after days of apparent coma, begins to stir on his bed and to show signs of struggle, the physician and the family rejoice. Struggle is life and life is hope. As in the physical, so in the moral life. *Natural Law in the Spiritual World* is the title of an old-fashioned book by Henry Drummond. It's a good phrase. There are endless analogies between the life of the body and that of the soul. The old definition of man as "a rational animal" does not mean, says an excellent writer, Dom Aelred Graham, that man is a "heterogeneous mixture" like, for example, oil and water. The rational and the animal in man need not always be contrasted; they may be compared and likened one with the other.

Well then, just as the writhings and squirmings of a sick man are a sign that he lives and still may live, so when a man's soul is battling with itself, we know that he is spiritually alive. It is a commonplace of spiritual doctrine—you may find it in any one of hundreds of books dealing with religion—that if a man has no temptations it must be that he is morally dead. Or, as some of the older and severer writers say, if he has ceased to fight, the devil already has him.

In a bitterly contested political campaign, the friends of one candidate for the United States Senate said, "Everybody likes him; he hasn't an enemy in the world." "Remarkable," answered the rival candidate. "But what has he been doing all these years in the Senate, that battleground of ideas and policies and conflicting forces? Has he slept through it all?" Shrewd enough. It recalls to mind the old recipe for being at peace with all the world, "Say nothing, do nothing, be nothing." "It's a good trick," as they say, "if you can do it." But to make no enemies wouldn't be a good trick even if you could do it. John the Baptist couldn't do it. Christ Himself couldn't do it. And we have it on His authority that the people killed all the prophets sent to them from God. And He explains: "If you have been of the world, the world would love its own; but because you are not of the world . . . therefore the world hateth you. It hath hated Me before you."

But as I have said, we are not now concerned about the fight of a man with the external foe. St. Augustine, and we with him, are discussing the enemy within the gates, the enemy under the same roof with us, yes, inside the same skin with us. "A man's enemies shall be they of his own household," says our Lord. Yes and closer to him than that. The member of a man's household that does him more harm than all others within or without is himself.

Persecutors seize a man, and as a preliminary to torture and death they throw him into a dungeon, chain him to the floor, and leave him alone, alone with his own worst enemy, himself. In solitary confinement, in the dark and the damp, all but starved and famished, ridden with vermin, crawled over and gnawed upon by rats, it is expected that he will weaken, recant, belie himself, repudiate his principles; that he will call for the guard and cry: "Take me out; I will sign any document; I will swear any oath; I will abjure my religion; I will offer incense to Caesar or to Jupiter. Only release me from this 'durance vile.'"

Obviously the enemy of that man is not the judge, or the State, or the jailers, or the torturers; not starvation or vermin; not the vision of the gallows or of the block; not fear of being crucified or burned alive or thrown to the beasts. His enemy is himself. When they threw him into that dark hole there commenced the inner battle, himself fighting himself. That battle is the one he lost. Other men have been apprehended, jailed, chained, left alone, but have remained true to their principles and to themselves. Nothing outside a man defiles a man, says Jesus; and nothing outside a man defeats a man. Defeat is from within.

St. Thomas More cast down from the eminence of the chancellery, first position in the realm after the king, left to languish in the Tower of London, endured the discomforts of that gloomy dungeon reeking not only with the filth of five centuries but with the memories of a thousand victims of angry kings and of hundreds of martyrs. Day after day with cunning cruelty his torturers sent in to him members of his own family to plead with him, to coax and tease him, to adjure him to put an end to what seemed to them an obstinate insistence upon a point of minor theological importance. The importunity of those who loved him was the most poignant of all his griefs. But he overcame them all because he had overcome himself.

But to return to that other saint, that other hero of the moral life in whose battle with himself we are now particularly interested, St. Augustine. I have referred time and again to the little masterpiece, his *Confessions,* and if only to prove to those who have not dug into that mine of literary and dramatic power and beauty that my enthusiasm is not excessive, I wish it were possible to repeat here all of the seventh and eighth and eleventh chapters in the Eighth Book of the *Confessions.* On the other hand I would not dare paraphrase those brilliant and eloquent passages any more than I would venture to put in my own words a speech of Hamlet or Macbeth or Coriolanus. So I find myself in a dilemma, which to be frank, I don't know how to resolve. But perhaps a fragment here and there from the incomparable original may not do the master too great injustice.

For twelve years he had been gradually approaching the crisis in his moral life. He had commenced not with the Gospels, for though his mother St. Monica was a Catholic, his father, whose name by the way was Patricius (Patrick), was a pagan, and Augustine at least in his youth had more of the pagan than of the Christian in him. Not the Gospels, then, but the *Hortensius* of Cicero, a treatise of which no copy remains, was his first incentive to philosophy and, by the same token, to virtue. "Not to sharpen my tongue did I pore over that book," he says. From the day that he opened it he "looked upon wisdom as the supreme goal of human endeavor." Then the battle began and lasted more than a decade of years. Encouragement, discouragement, illusion, disillusion, hopes, high expectations of discovering the truth, cruel disappointments, succeeded one another in rapid succession, or to speak more accurately, accompanied one another. And all the while, as if his intellectual problem were not excruciating enough, there was the ugly horrible battle with carnal passion, incessant, importunate, absorbing, devastating. A less heroic man would have succumbed and abandoned the struggle for truth. If he had surrendered he would perhaps have become reprobate. But though beaten down by doubt and by his vicious propensities, he was made of stern moral stuff. He was a valiant fighter and a persistent seeker.

Twelve years of that, and then the climax. "There was a garden to our lodging," he says, "of which we had the use. Thither the tumult of my breast drove me where no one could interrupt the duel into which I had entered with myself . . . I was mad, unto salvation, I was dying, unto life . . . I was groaning in spirit, shaken with a gust of indignation because I could not enter into Thy will, O my God, yet all my bones were crying out that this was the way . . . How did I reproach myself! with what sharp reasons did I flog my soul to make it follow me in my effort to follow Thee. And it would not; it refused and would not even make an excuse. All its arguments had been tried and found wanting, yet it resisted in sullen disquiet, fearing as if it were death, the closing of that running sore of evil habit by which it was being wasted to death."

"Thou, O Lord, wast urgent in my inmost heart, plying with austere mercy the scourges of fear and shame . . . I kept saying within myself, 'O let it be now, let it be now.' I was on the verge of resolution. I did not slip back. I stood close and took fresh breath. I tried again and came a little nearer. I could all but touch and reach my goal, but I did not quite reach or touch it . . . Trifles of trifles and vanities held me back: they caught hold of the garment of my flesh and whispered in my ear, 'Can you let us go . . . from that instant this and that will be forbidden you.' What did they mean, O my God, what did they mean by '*this* and *that*'? O let Thy mercy guard the soul of Thy servant from the vileness, the shame that they meant."

So, the magnificent passage continues until he comes to the next of his talk: "Such was the debate that raged in my heart, myself battling against myself." The dramatic denouement of that inward struggle all the world knows. "I flung myself down under a fig tree," he says, "and gave my tears free course and the floods of my eyes broke forth . . . I cried unto Thee O Lord incessantly, How long, O Lord, how long! . . . Tomorrow and tomorrow?"

Augustine wrestling with himself in the garden at Milan is

like Jacob wrestling with the angel and saying, "I will not let thee go except thou bless me."

Suddenly, cutting across the interior tumult, a voice is heard, like that of children playing: *"Tolle Lege, Tolle Lege."* "Take and read, take and read." "I stemmed the rush of tears," he says, "and rose to my feet . . . I ran back to the place where I had left a volume of the Apostle (Paul). I caught it up, opened it, and read in silence the passage on which my eyes first fell, 'Not in rioting and drunkenness, not in chambering and wantonness, not in strife and envying, but put ye on the Lord Jesus Christ and make not provision for the flesh to fulfill the lusts thereof.' "

The battle was over. Victory had been won. "No further would I read," he says, "nor was it necessary." "We went in," he continued (he and his friend Alypius), "to my mother and to her great joy told her what had happened."

No one is prepared for the full meaning and value of that conversion who has not followed the great penitent through the first seven books of his *Confessions*. So perhaps I might better have said merely *"Tolle Lege,"* "Take and Read." Read the book, but read the heart of the man. Read your own heart in the light of the revelation he has made of his. If a man must say what Louis XIV said when a great preacher had touched his heart, *C'est moi, C'est moi*—"He speaks of me, He speaks of me," the struggle is not Augustine's alone but mine; I too know that heart-rendering experience of 'myself battling myself.' The outcome of that struggle will be the same as the conclusion of his. "O Lord, I am Thy servant and the son of Thy hand-maid. Thou hast burst my bands asunder: to Thee will I offer the sacrifice of praise. Let my heart and my tongue praise Thee. Let them speak and do Thou answer and say unto my soul, 'I am Thy Salvation.' "

Chapter 6

"Too Late Have I Loved Thee"

WE OFTEN say that men of genius live under the spell of a consuming passion. A philosopher like Socrates in ancient times or like Immanuel Kant in a more recent day is so completely absorbed in the pursuit of wisdom that he ignores or despises most of the things that the worldly-minded think important. To the philosopher, ambition, for example, is nonsense; a hankering for position and power, childish; the accumulation of money, ridiculous. His passion is learning; the desire of his heart is for wisdom and truth.

So too the poet the artist the musician have an all-absorbing passion, the love of beauty. The poet desires above all things to capture and transmit some fleeting vision he has had of the glory and beauty of the world about him or within him. He sings of the vision of beauty without or within: "I have so loved thee, but cannot hold thee; fading like a dream the shadows fold thee." We have, all of us, looked with a kind of minor ecstasy upon a gorgeous sunset. We have felt a gentle sadness when the colors upon the clouds lost their brilliance. But the poet and the painter are not content to behold and to be sad; they feel a determination to try to capture and to perpetuate that burst of heavenly beauty, that preview of eternal glory. They work at high speed and in a fine frenzy to write it down or to put it on canvas. "Stay, thou art so fair," they cry.

Also, the composer of noble music is enraptured by harmonies that sing themselves in his heart. He digs them out of their hiding place and attempts to share them with his fellows. It may be that he leaps from his bed where the melodies have come to him, whether in a dream or a reverie, and he jots them down in what we call notes of music on a scale. Artists all live at high tension, in a kind of intermittent fever. When their inspiration is at its peak, they are lost, absorbed, consumed in the fire of a great passion. Like the poet, or the painter, or the musician, a crusader for social justice is devoured with a passion not for what is artistically but for what is morally beautiful. Abraham Lincoln, Samuel Wilberforce, Bartholomew de las Casas, William Lloyd Garrison, St. Vincent de Paul were as much on fire to make men see the good as Beethoven, Brahms and Tschaikovsky, Dante, Keats and Shelley and Francis Thompson, with the desire to make men see the beautiful, or Socrates and St. Thomas Aquinas to communicate wisdom and truth.

Now the great passion that burned in the heart of St. Augustine was not for poetry or music or art or philosophic thought, but for God. To him all that is True and Beautiful and Good were summed up in God. It is commonly said of a certain philosopher, Spinoza, that he was "God-intoxicated." Perhaps so, but the philosopher who above all others was entranced, enraptured, and uplifted in a kind of perpetual ecstasy by the thought and the presence and the realization of God, was St. Augustine. Here and there in literature you find an apostrophe to the stars or to the sea or to Mont Blanc or to Man, but *The Confessions of St. Augustine* are one long sustained apostrophe to God. He speaks to God in more impassioned language than ever lover spoke to his beloved. In almost any chapter of that continuous prose-poem you may find an outburst of thanks and praise and love to God. The passage from which the title of this chapter is taken is only one among a hundred.

"Too late have I loved Thee, O Beauty ever ancient ever new, too late have I come to love Thee. Behold, Thou wert within me, and I without; and there made I search for Thee; wrongly I cast myself upon the things of Thy creation which yet Thou hadst made so fair. Thou wert with me indeed but I was not with Thee. Those things withheld me from Thee. But Thou didst call and cry out to me, and Thou didst break through the barrier of my deafness, 'Coruscasti, splenduisti, fugastis caecitatem meam:' Thou didst flash Thy lightnings before me, Thy splendor burst upon me, and Thou didst put my blindness to flight. Thou didst breathe Thy fragrance upon me, and I drew in my breath; yet do I sigh after Thee. I tasted Thee and still I hunger and thirst for more. Thou didst but touch me, and I do burn with a desire to enjoy Thee."

Evidently the God whom St. Augustine loved so passionately is not the God of the philosophers. Learned men in all ages, pagans, Jews, Christians, even those that think themselves un-believers, yes cynics, skeptics, scoffers (one of these last being Voltaire), have set themselves to prove the existence of God— of a God—and they have demonstrated beyond preadventure of doubt a Supreme Being, a First Cause, Prime Mover, Alpha and Omega, the Beginning and the End of all things, a Life Force. But Cardinal Newman says of such argumentation: "I am far from denying the real force of the arguments in proof of a God, drawn from the general facts of human society and the course of history, but these do not warm me or enlighten me; they do not take away the winter of my desolation, or make the buds unfold and the leaves grow within me and my moral being re-joice."

St. Augustine was a philosopher, a supreme philosopher, but he could never have been warmed or enlightened by the philoso-pher's God. No "Supreme Being," or "First Cause," or "Prime Mover," still less "The Great Mathematician," as a scientist has called Him, or the "Architect of the Universe" of the ritual of Freemasonry—no such God could have elicited from Augustine such ardent expressions of personal love as you find in the Con-fessions.

Nor is the God of poets or artists or of the creators of music the God of Augustine. He asks: "When I love Thee, what is it that I love? Not the beauty of any body, not the order of time, not the clearness of this light that so gladdens our eyes, not the harmony of sweet songs of every kind, not the fragrancy of flowers, or spices of aromatical odours, not manna, nor honey, nor limbs delightful to the embrace of flesh and blood. Not these things do I love, in loving my God. Yet do I love a kind of light, a kind of voice, a kind of odour, a kind of food, and a kind of embracing, when I love my God, Who is the light, the voice, the odour, the food, the embracing of my inward man; where that Light shineth into my soul which is not circumscribed by any place, when that voice soundeth which is not snatched away by time, when that odour pours forth which is not scattered by the air, when that food savours the taste which is unconsumed by eating, when that embracement is enjoyed which is not divorced by satiety. This it is which I love, when I love my God."

It must be admitted that such impassioned language as this sounds unreal to those who have no God at all, or who, believing in God, have no intimate contact with Him. There are those to whom God is so remote as to be in effect non-existent. They say they believe in Him, but they do not love Him, at least not with a glowing flaming love like that of the saints. Even in our churches when the congregation sings to God, "I love Thee so I know not how my transports to control, Thy love is like a burning fire within my inmost soul," the sentiment is not truly their own. It came from the tongue or pen of some mystic saint. They read it and sing it, but it is not theirs. If you stop them in the midst of a strophe of one of these impassioned love songs to God, and ask, "Do you *mean* that?," they may suddenly awake to a sense of the unreality of their devotion and confess: "How can I? How can anyone? How can I love God whom I cannot even see?"

If on the other hand you were to approach a poet who has written some highly passionate lyric and ask him, "Do you really feel such perfervid emotion"; or if you were to challenge the composer of some transcendentally beautiful and deeply moving music and ask, "Are these your genuine sentiments or are they only a beautiful fiction; are you not claiming the poets' privilege of hyperbole?" the poet or the musician would answer: "I have been able to express only a faint semblance of the beauty of the vision I have seen, or of the enchanting harmonies I have heard in my soul. I would that my tongue could utter the thoughts that arise in me."

As with the poet or the musician, so with the saint—so with a mystic like St. Augustine. If you or I were to suspect that the prose-poems of the love of God which he scatters so prodigally throughout the *Confessions* are nothing more than flights of fancy, a kind of artistic make-believe, if not sheer fantasy or perhaps religious hysteria, the saint would perhaps admit that he ought not to have tried to convey to others what took place between him and God in "the fields and caves and innumerable dens," as he says, in the secret recesses of his inner self. But he will go on to explain that he was driven, like the poet, the painter, the sculptor, the composer, by an impulse that could not be denied; and he will insist that what he has put upon paper is not an infinitesimal part of what he has felt. In a very familiar hymn St. Bernard, who was as great a poet as he was a saint, wrote "nor voice can sing, nor heart can frame, nor can the memory find" words in which to speak the love of God. Why then does the saint try to sing it, to say it, to put it into words and write it? Because his heart would break and his soul would suffocate if he did not find some outlet for the passion within him.

Indeed, words and sounds and color and form such as the poets and other artists use to convey their spiritual experience to the outside world are but clumsy instruments. There remained much more poetry in the heart of Shakespeare and Shelley than ever came out; Dante did not succeed in revealing to us what he had seen either in the *Inferno* or the *Paradiso*. Raphael tried all through a long lifetime to put on canvas his ideal of the Madonna, but the Madonna in the mind was always more beautiful than the Madonna on canvas. St. Teresa, commanded to write her mystical experience in what is called rather oddly her autobiography, wept and groaned and expostulated that there are no words to express such matters.

So of St. Augustine. He felt not less than he has said of the love of God, but more. He, above all others, recognized that when you really come into contact with the Infinite Beauty that is God you must be silent. The Catholic mystical theology teaches that in the flight to the Divine all things of earth must be left behind, not only worldly pleasures and comforts, not only sins and vices, but even one's own very self. Among the things that must be left behind are words and sounds. St. Francis de Sales says that when the soul communicates with God in mystic love, "She speaks not, she sighs not, she breathes not, she prays not." All must be silent without and within. St. Augustine in what is perhaps at once the most beautiful and the best known passage in his *Confessions* relates that as he and his mother, St. Monica, were together at Ostia, waiting to take ship to Africa, they fell to wondering about heaven. "We asked ourselves," he says, "in the presence of Thee O God, the Truth, what will be the manner of eternal life . . . Sweet was the converse we held together" as "we attempted to attain some poor conception of that glorious theme." "We soared," he continues, "with glowing hearts towards Thee, mounting step by step the ladder of the material order through the heavens themselves. Still higher did we climb, and so we came to our own minds and passed beyond them . . . And we said, if the tumult of the flesh were hushed; hushed these shadows of earth, sea, sky; hushed the heavens and the soul itself, so that it should pass beyond itself and not think of itself; if all dreams were hushed, and all sensuous revelations, and every tongue and every symbol; if all that comes and goes were hushed." All these things in the heavens and on earth speak their message and are silent, he says, and then the beholder is uplifted and transported, leaving them all behind, to behold and to be enraptured by the Beauty from which they all proceed.

Now here is the difference between the saint and any poet or musician who looks upon created beauty as an end in itself. The saint commences with beautiful ideas or sights or sounds, but passes through them above and beyond them to Uncreated Beauty, that is to God. All poetry and art and music are vain if they do not prompt the hearer or the beholder to leave the poem or the painting or the music behind and pass beyond to the Infinite Beauty of which they are only fragmentary symbols. Great art cannot leave you where it finds you. If it stops at the canvas, if it is contained within the frame, it is not great art. It must enable and indeed compel you to forget color and form and composition and pass beyond. Music must lift you out of this tangible audible world and waft you away as on a magic carpet to the world where there is no longer any sound. Otherwise it is not great music.

Now the saint knows this. To him a thing of beauty is not a joy forever. Rather like the rainbow it comes and goes, or like the rose it blooms and dies. All beauty that passes is pathetic, but it has served its purpose if it has led the soul to the Beauty that never fades, the Beauty that is God. There is, then, Beauty which the poet and the artist and the music-maker try to clutch with their hands, and bring down to earth. Sometimes they succeed; sometimes they fail; often they know not how near they are to the Infinite Source of all Beauty. But the saint has the advantage over the artist. He says; "I know in Whom I have believed." He knows, and, knowing, laments that he has not always known. When once he has laid hold of God and possesses Him, he exclaims what we shall all cry out to God when first our eyes are opened really to behold Him: "Too late have I known Thee, O Beauty ever ancient, ever new. Too late have I come to know Thee."

PART III

GOD AND NO GOD

Chapter 7

The "Liberation" of Man

EVERY philosophy that offers itself as a substitute for religion appeals to man in the name of freedom. Religion—so runs the argument—is by definition a relationship between God and man. But God—also by definition—is infinite and man finite. God is omniscient and all-powerful, man weak and ignorant, God transcendent, man earth bound, and so on through the list of attributes of God and of man. How then, can there be between the All and the nothing any relationship but that of abasement of one before the other? And is abasement a "relationship?"

So philosophical atheism calls upon man to free himself from God. "Man is by nature free but he is everywhere in chains," says the atheist, borrowing a slogan from Rousseau. But whereas Communism holds that man has been put in chains by capitalism, the atheist asserts that the chains have been forged by man himself. God did not make man, says the atheist, but man made God; made Him out of nothing—nothing but his own fears, superstitions, illusions, hallucinations. So, says the atheist to man—borrowing once again—"You have nothing to lose but your chains." The chains, furthermore, are imaginary. You can throw them off by thinking them off.

It sounds plausible but of course it is nonsense. But before setting the atheist right on the question of religion as slavery, let us note the fact that in his eagerness to get rid of God he discloses a strange concept of man. G. K. Chesterton, in answer to the charge that the Church is too soft and again too savage, too indulgent and too tolerant, too submissive and too aggressive, says it is possible for a man to be too fat in one place and too thin in another, but "He would be a queer shape." Man, as imagined by the atheist, is a queer shape. He knows enough to make God but having made God he doesn't know that he has made Him. The potter doesn't know that he has made the vase, the architect that he has designed the house, the poet that he has written the poem. Man makes God and then bows down before the work of his own hands. There is indeed something of this in Isaias, who speaks with scorn of the idolator who cuts down the tree, makes kindling wood of part of it but with the remainder makes an idol and prays to it "Thou art my God." But Isaias spoke of barbarians. The atheist forgets that the race at large has progressed out of barbarism and that the further it has advanced, the more it has developed and purified its idea of God. Andrew M. Fairbairn in his *Philosophy of the Christian Religion,* written many years ago but by no means outdated, says:

"Man may have started on his new career as a being with a capacity for religion, one who feared powers invisible impersonated in a blasted tree, a rude stone, a whitened bone, or a running stream, but he has not stood fixed in that rude faith . . . he has come to think of a God majestic, sole, holy, ineffable, who inhabiteth eternity."

Someone should present to the atheist's frustrated intellect the fact that belief in God is not confined to savages and imbeciles. Men of acute and profound intelligence believe in God. I have read many attacks upon God, but they all seem to be concerned with some Mumbo Jumbo god, never with the God of Aquinas, Sir Isaac Newton, John Henry Newman, Blaise Pascal, or of any other great mind. It is as though one were to call for the abolition of music because he loathes boogie-woogie, or for the proscription of art because he finds cubism unnatural and "abstract" art puzzling. I have my own *bête noire,* philosophers who practise the cult of unintelligibility, but I would not on that account propose the death penalty for all philosophers. If there were no God but the God of the aborigines, we would all be in favor of abolishing religion. But there is another God.

However we were saying that the atheist, in his eagerness to abolish God, underrates man. To produce so stupendous a concept as that of a Being infinitely powerful, all knowing, and— be it added though the atheist ignores these attributes: all good, all holy, all wise, all merciful—to conceive such a noble idea, even if it were only an idea, demands high intelligence. And how could man who has shown such intelligence be at the same time so imbecile as not to know that the idea he has of God is of his own creating? A man too fat in one place and too thin in another is possible. But can man be both a genius and a dolt? If man is that sort of anomaly and has been so for millenniums, does the atheist think him amenable to correction at this late date?

What ails the atheist among other things is that he has never taken the pains—perhaps he has not the capacity—to understand what St. Paul tried to tell "certain philosophers of the Epicureans and the Stoics" at Athens: "He (God) giveth to all life and breath and all things . . . in Him we live and move and have our being." The modern philosophical atheist who asks man to free himself from God doesn't understand that God is man's element. To ask him to rid himself of God is like asking the fish to free itself from the sea, the bird from the air. Nor can the atheist rise to the concept that God is the source of Life, Truth, Justice, Love, all that is Good. Like those who, as St. Jude says, "blaspheme whatever things they know not," he rails at some anthropomorphic substitute for God.

As for the perverse notion that man created God out of nothing, the historical fact is that man believes in God for the same reason that he believes that the Sphinx was not made by the winds blowing upon the sands of Egypt or that the Taj

Mahal and the dome of St. Peter's "just happened." Nothing just happens, least of all the Universe. Let us give man credit for at least a glimmer of intelligence. No man, except the atheist, believes that a non-existent universe said to its non-existent self on some bright non-existent morning, "I shall now exist." There are limits to the imbecility of this poor human race of ours, atheists, even philosophical atheists, to the contrary notwithstanding.

Père Charles in one of many happy similes in his *Prayer for All Times,* speaks of an echo that denies the voice that made it, and the image which denies the object of which it is the reflection. No voice, no echo; no object, no image; no God, no man. "I could sooner deny my own existence," said John Henry Newman, "than deny the existence of God."

Atheism is not always philosophical or metaphysical. More often it is ethical—or anti-ethical. Man, says the atheist, created not only a God and a religion; he created the idea—the illusion —of sin. And the notion of sin has caused poor man more anguish and has been a greater hindrance to the progress of the race than the idea of God. So, says the atheist, let us rid man of this second bugaboo.

Now I am not concerned with proving that sin is no illusion, any more than I was concerned above with proving that God exists. In this essay I suggest that we consider what the atheist does to man by way of "liberating" him. For a parallel we might consider what organized atheism has done to the captive countries which it has "liberated." But that would lead us too far astray.

In order to get rid of sin the "liberator" says we must first deny freedom of the will and hence moral responsibility. Now it may be possible for the atheist to believe that by making man an automaton or an animal he exalts man, but to us Christians it is freedom of choice that makes man. "Behold I have set before you good and evil, heaven and hell," says God to man;

"Choose ye therefore." Such freedom is magnificent or terrible or both but it is freedom. If to relieve man of the "illusion" of sin one must deny the distinguishing mark that separates man from the brute, the denial is equivalent to a recommendation that man commit mental and moral suicide. The denial of free will in man makes him something less than man, all philosophical, scientific, psychiatric jargon notwithstanding.

It is said that Voltaire, hearing some one dogmatically deny the existence of hell said, "I wish I could be as sure about that as you seem to be." A man may say "I wish I could believe that I am not responsible for what I do," but there remains the still small voice within which tells him that good is good and bad is bad, and not all the specious argumentation in the world can rid him of that certainty. "There are more things in heaven and earth Horatio, than are dreamed of in your philosophy." And there are more things in the heart of man than are recognized by certain philosophies and certain brands of "science."

So, the denial of God and of sin, though intended to exalt man, debases him. We had better hold on to the old philosophies until a new one comes along that is more worthy of man than ours.

Chapter 8

Atheism in Theory

WHEN a clergyman confronts the subject, "Atheism," the chances are a thousand to one that he will launch forth upon a proof of the existence of God. This time I follow a different procedure. Proof of the existence of God is wasted on those who are perverse enough to deny God. King David in the *Book of Psalms* spoke none too vigorously: "Only the fool hath said in his heart 'There is no God'." Cardinal Newman says that the existence of God is as plain as one's own existence. If any man question that fact, set him the task of explaining how there can be a man if there be no God. In fact you can embarrass him quite as much if you ask him to explain the origin of anything, a grain of sand, a drop of water, a speck of dust, an atom of hydrogen or what you will. You need not quite overwhelm him by demanding to know how the oceans, the mountain ranges, the dome of heaven with its incomputable number of universes, came into being. Give the poor fellow not an ocean to explain but a pebble on the shore of the ocean, not the Milky Way, but only as much star dust as you could pick up on the point of a needle. Then sit back and watch him squirm and strain as he wrestles with the real Riddle of the Universe: How did something, anything, come out of nothing? Don't let him wander; don't let him orate, don't let him deceive you with pseudo-scientific verbiage; don't let him throw dust into the air unless he first explains where he got the dust and the air.

Almost all atheists seem to imagine that a group of theologians met together in secret session and said to one another, "Let us concoct a dogma and impose it on the people." And lo, they came forth from the hall of conspiracy with a formula which they taught men, women, and children, to say: "I believe in God." But the theologians didn't invent God. Man—simple man, not perhaps the man in the street for there weren't any streets, but the man in the woods, the man on the mountain, the man under the starry sky, the man on the shore of the sea—came to the instant conclusion that there must be a God, for the self-same reason and by the same instinctive logic as Robinson Crusoe came to the swift realization that there must be a man on the island because he saw a human foot-print. God didn't make the world, couldn't make the world, without leaving all over it hints, suggestions, tell-tale evidence that He had been here. "The heavens shew forth the glory of God," says the Psalmist, "and the firmament declareth His handiwork." Man, primitive man, as yet unsoiled with curious, intricate, impossible philosophies, had a firm grasp on the fundamental principle of science: "Nothing comes from nothing; whatever is made had a maker."

It is significant that after Immanuel Kant had rejected that simple reasoning as proof of the existence of God, his disciples went straight on from where he left off and rejected it as proof of the existence of man. "If any man," said Cardinal Manning, "pretends to doubt his own existence, he is trifling with me," but the logical outcome of the denial of God's existence is the denial of one's own existence. And that, I think, is what the other great English Cardinal, John Henry Newman, had in mind when he said, "The Being of God is as certain to me as the certainty of my own existence."

However, I don't intend to follow that line of thought. I am going to embarrass the atheist in the most effective way possible: by agreeing with him. For the sake of the argument I am going to give up the argument. I surrender; I yield, lock, stock and barrel. The atheist is right; there is no God. Then what? "Then

what?" echoes the atheist; "Then nothing. We're through." The
atheist may be through, but I am not. My mind refuses to stop
dead and cease to function when some one cries "Finis," as a
horse stops when his master says "Whoa!" The mind of man is
a contrary animal. If one tells me that there is no God and that
is all, that this is the end of the mental process on the subject,
my mind rebels, becomes fractious. Instead of stopping or slow-
ing down, it runs on with leaps and bounds, trying to answer
the question "What then?"

The difficulty is that God has so woven Himself into the warp
and woof of civilization; has so built Himself into the fabric
of human institutions; has so deeply ensconced Himself in the
heart and mind of man, in our thoughts and affections, our
manners and habits and customs, that you can't get rid of God
without setting the whole world askew, without wrenching the
heart of man and emptying his life of almost all that it contains.
It would be a mistake to imagine that if God goes, nothing
happens but that churches fall into ruins and priests perish. A
great many more institutions than churches depend upon the
fact of God. I don't mean merely schools, colleges, hospitals,
orphan asylums, and multitudes of other appendages of religion.
I mean courts of justice, bulwarks of law and order; I mean
nations, governments, and all humanitarian organizations; I
mean the family, the nucleus of society, and society itself; I mean
art and music and literature—understand, not merely "Christian"
art, Giotto and Mantegna and Raphael and Leonardo and
Michelangelo, not merely primitive art or the art of the Renais-
sance, but *all* art; not merely sacred music, the austere chant
of the Church and the polyphony of Palestrina, but Mozart and
Liszt and Brahms and Beethoven; I mean *all* music; not merely
religious literature, the psalms of David, the book of Job, the
prophets and the Gospels; I mean *all* literature. And when I say
colleges I don't mean Catholic colleges or denominational col-

leges; I mean *all* colleges and all universities, all education, all culture, all civilization.

I hope that no one will think it necessary to remind me that art and music and literature are produced by men who profess no belief in God, and that educational institutions exist in which God is ignored or ridiculed or rejected. Nor need I be told that there are men who either neglect or refuse to pray, but who nonetheless live what is usually called a moral life. But these persons are one and all worshippers of God. God is the True, the Good, and the Beautiful. Whoever seeks the Truth or loves the Good, or strives in prose or in verse, in bronze, in marble, on canvas, or through the insubstantial ethereal, elusive, evanescent medium of melody and harmony, to express the Beautiful, is really, though he know it not, striving for God. The flower is not aware that it turns to the sun, the river doesn't know that it rushes to the sea, the entire universe plunging along through space at inconceivable speed, is not aware that it is progressing towards a Goal. And so man, who should know, may not know that in the very attempt to produce poetry or art or music he is seeking God. If the atheist could indeed exile God from the Universe, with God would go all Beauty, all Good, all Truth. I will not say that these things accompany God into exile, for they are not accompaniments of God; they are the essence of God. If God goes they go, just as inevitably as body and soul, the essence of man, go wherever man goes.

The atheist may imagine that when God goes, "Thou shalt not kill, and Thou shalt not steal" will remain behind. They can no more remain than the smile on the face of the Cheshire cat can remain after the cat is gone. Men may talk of a naturalistic ethics, ethics based on reason alone, and there may be such an ethics for Seneca or Marcus Aurelius or Epictetus, or Ralph Waldo Emerson or Henry Thoreau. But your naturalistic ethics simply won't do for the mass of mankind. If you say to the ordinary man, "Thou shalt Not!", he answers "Says Who?" If you reply "Epictetus!" or "Hammurabi," or "Lao Tse," he will laugh in your face. Even if you refer the Commandments to Moses, that too will be ineffective. For mankind at large (and I don't mind admitting that includes *me* and I dare say *you*) there is only one sanction that is in the last analysis valid. "Thus sayeth the Lord, the Lord God, Judge of the Living and the Dead, the Awful Infinite Ruler of our Eternal Destiny." Remove that final sanction and you tear down the fabric of society. Tear down the fabric? Say rather tear up the foundations.

For those who love bare hard cold logic, I present the argument in skeleton form: No God, No Law of God, all law is of man; if all law is of man, why should man obey? Must I, a man, bend my head and crook my knee to another man? Not if I *am* a man. Do you tell me: not to another man but to a body of men. To a legislature? To an aggregation of moral philosophers? To a board of university professors of the science of ethics? To some socio- logical society? But to us, or to any independent thinker, what competency on morality has a legislature which can be packed with certain mental and moral mediocrities, low grade politicians whose only virtue is "regularity." Do you think to capture my intelligence and compel my will by the mandates of such a legislature?

Or with some more pretentious group of self-styled humani- tarians, or professors of moral philosophy? But I think I would rather obey a low-brow legislature than a highbrow university body. There is a chance that the legislature, though composed of men of mediocre mentality, might still retain some modicum of common sense, but your university group would very likely be in favor of a variety of fantastic ethical monstrosities. The people at large maintain whatever degree of moral sanity they have, be- cause they recognize the absurdity and the immorality of their would-be mentors from the universities.

Let's delay no more upon this point. Here and now I declare my conviction and, I believe the conviction of millions of my fellowmen, not all of us being unintelligent: if there is no divine sanction behind a human law, I feel myself free to disobey that law whenever and however I please. In my morality as in my religion, I refuse like the Israelites to bend the knee to Baal. Baal, you understand, was a false god, an intruder in the place of the true God. So, any law-making body, any group of men high or low, philosophical or political, that pretends to take the place of God, commands my obedience, and limits my liberty as a substitute for a banished God, is to me a usurper and a blasphemer. I would then no more obey a senate and a house, or any court, high or low, than I would conform to the behavior-maxims of Confucius, or the moral mandates of Zoroaster. If there be no law of God I will not obey the law of man, because the only reason I now obey the law of man is that I admit it to be an expression of the law of God.

But I have a wider and deeper problem for the atheist. If he takes God away from man, he must give man something to take the place of God. Taking away God leaves an enormous vacuum not only in the world but in the human heart. You might better take the sun out of the heavens or the earth from under man's feet than take away his God. Again and again we quote that profound and utterly true sentence of St. Augustine," Thou hast made us for Thyself, O God, and our hearts are restless until they find rest in Thee." At first hearing that utterance sounds mystical, but it is not mere mysticism; it is in epitome the history of man. It may seem at first blush theological, but it is really psychological. Nothing satisfies the human heart but God. True, in times of decadence as it is written, "The people sat down to eat, and drink, and they rose up to play." There are rollicking songs about "Wine, women, and song," and there was the cry of the degenerate mob in the days of the later Caesars, *Panem et circenses!* "Give us food and entertainment!" But did not the wisest of Men say, "Man doth not live by bread alone"? If man were content and happy when filled with food, or for that matter wine; if he sought no further joy than the satisfaction of lust; if a house and a home and a family could answer all his requirements; if he would even be satisfied when surfeited with riches or with power, the history of our race would have been much more ignoble than it is. But man has always hungered and thirsted for something besides meat and drink, and though he does, to his shame, seem for awhile to be content with the base pleasures of the flesh, they don't satisfy him for long. His most important craving is for intangible, immaterial, spiritual things. Otherwise there would have been no art, no music, no poetry, no high literature, no culture, no civilization. Indeed if you seek another axiomatic utterance as profound, as beautiful, and as true as that of St. Augustine, you have it in the 41st Psalm;—"As the hart panteth after the fountains of water, so my Soul panteth after Thee, O God. My Soul hath thirsted after the strong living God . . . My tears have been my bread day and night, whilst it is said to me daily: Where is thy God."

There is no wisdom in quarreling with that trait of human nature. One who finds fault with an elementary passion of the human heart, denies it and attempts to frustrate it, is guilty of unnatural crime. But the sin and the blunder, the crime of atheism is that it attempts to tear out of the heart of man his craving for the spiritual, his hunger and thirst for the Infinite, and that it gives, and can give, no substitute for God and religion.

The true God being abolished, men turn to sticks and stones in place of God. They have worshipped a sacred bull, a cat, a crocodile, a black stone fallen from the heavens. They have even been guilty of the unspeakable depravity of worshipping a Nero or a Domitian or even Domitian's horse. We have seen in our own day that since the Russian peasants were forbidden to worship God they have filed in a never ending procession into the tomb of Lenin in Moscow to worship (for that is what it means, it is not a mere pathological curiosity: it is religion) to worship an embalmed body of a man who hated most of his fellow-men, slaughtered the helpless imperial family, father, mother, and children, like so many sheep in a shambles, deluged his own country in blood, erected and perpetuated the most galling tyranny the world has ever seen, and left behind him as a legacy the command to conquer the world in the name of class hatred. A pretty god indeed, but that is the kind of god you get when you abolish the good God.

Chapter 9

Atheism In Practice

Now that a system of atheism has been set up and put into operation over a vast territory in Europe and Asia, it is possible to see how atheism works. It was never possible before. There has not been until now a specimen of pure undiluted atheism on a national or international scale. It is doubtful if there ever was even one man who consistently lived by his professed atheism. We have indeed, had persons who declared themselves to have no God, but none of them ever had the courage to "follow through" with that denial. All so-called atheists are—admit it or not—beneficiaries of religion. Religion is part of their heritage. It has come to them through the blood of many generations of ancestors. Like the multitudes who never pray or join in public worship, they do nothing to increase their heritage or pass it on. But they enjoy its benefits none the less. They are not really good examples of what atheism can do.

So too with governments, our own included. The United States of America has been officially declared a Christian nation. But we don't always act Christian. Sometimes we do and again we do not. Our national action, like our individual action, is spotty as far as religion and morality are concerned. So America is not really a good example of Christianity in action.

Neither are the governments really atheist that from time to time go on an atheistic binge. They cast out priests, tear down altars, destroy churches, put a ban on religious education, confiscate church property. The priests return, churches and schools are re-opened, at first surreptitiously, later with no attempt at concealment. Religion was driven underground, but not rooted out. It cannot be rooted out. "Atheist" governments do not, or hitherto have not, "meant business." They fight a battle but they don't wage a war against religion. There never has been and there never was intended to be a government or a nation permanently atheist. Sporadic attempts made on religion have a political purpose. They are not what they purport to be.

Religion which over the centuries has been woven into the fabric of all laws, constitutions, manners, customs, traditional practices, cannot be destroyed. If it could, nihilism would take over, and atheists don't want nihilism. After a brief experiment with atheism the French Revolution, for example, re-established a kind of religion. Robespierre made himself ridiculous by organizing and taking part in what was in effect, a religious ceremonial. Napoleon set things right again by sweeping atheism and atheist imitation of Catholicism clean off the board. Perhaps he had no more personal faith than Danton or Robespierre or D'Alembert, but he was not imbecile enough to imagine that a government could be run without God.

So until the Russian experiment we never have had on exhibition a *bona fide,* simon-pure, self-consistent atheism. As a matter of fact we haven't yet. The Soviets tolerate the continued existence of religious bodies—principally the Orthodox Church—provided they "co-operate" by cutting down their personnel and their services to an irreducible minimum and by slavish obedience to governmental decrees. But it is probably true to say that there never has been so nearly perfect an atheism as that now established in the U.S.S.R. and officially implemented over one-third of the population of the globe.

Hitherto atheism has been a theory, something academic, a philosophy arrived at by a dialectic process. Those who devised it and communicated it to college boys and girls had never tried it out *extra muros.* Atheism was a matter for the classroom, the lecture hall, the library. The professors—with the exception of one or two—did not go out into the market place to sell atheism to the people. They would have abhorred any such public propaganda. So they never knew, nor did we, how atheism would work if once it were let loose over a vast section of the globe. Now we know. Academic atheists, I imagine, are rather annoyed with Russia for having "shot the works." Atheism was attractive while it remained esoteric.

However, it is true that quietly and with every precaution of secrecy the professors presented their theory "where it would do the most good," in "liberal" and leftist periodicals. From there it was to seep down, not too quickly, to the general populace. Professors, like politicians, exercise a certain prudence, discretion, economy in communicating knowledge to the world at large. As every advertising agency knows, in these days of applied psychology, the people are to be conditioned before they are indoctrinated. They must be introduced gradually to a system of thought or action which seen at once and entirely would frighten them. Atheism—and Communism—to borrow Pope's line about vice, "is a monster of so frightful mien, As to be hated needs but to be seen."

The academicians had to a degree persuaded the learned world to which they belong that if and when man dismissed God from his thinking, his living, his law-making, there would be no decline in morals, personal or public, but that there would be an improvement. With belief in God, they said, civilization has reached its nadir. Without God it will be better, because when the bottom has been reached there is no way to go but up. Indeed, the City of God was to be demolished to make room for the City of Man.

But now that the most thoroughgoing attempt has been made for some forty years and on a vast scale the world knows what to think of that atheist prophecy. Atheistic Communism turns out to be the enemy of man as well as of God. In place of man in God's place we have Satan. With Satan we have a condition like that of Dante's Inferno, but worse because real not imaginary.

The leaders of this now existing Communist-atheist movement have been likened to "Chicago gangsters," a generic term used by Europeans to designate a brand of hoodlum-thug-killer. The comparison is wholly inadequate. No thug or gang of thugs in Chicago or anywhere else ever shot down in cold blood 10,000 soldiers and civilians in a day, as the Russians did in the Katyn Forest, or deliberately starved to death some 6 to 10 million harmless peasants as the Russians did in the Ukraine, or condemned uncounted millions to slave labor.

The reader must not suppose that I accept the professors' theory that Communism could have been less horrible in other hands than those of the Russians. Marxism is essentially evil. It denies the dignity of man as a child of God. Tell man that since the beginning, he has been under the delusion of grandeur in thinking himself the image of God; tell him that free will is a delusion and that there is no moral responsibility; persuade him that he is an animal, and he will set to work to prove your theory. You will cry out for the return of God even as a Beneficent Delusion.

Futhermore, Marxism calls for the re-formation of human society not by parliamentary method but by conspiracy, bloodshed, warfare, global revolution. For the accomplishment of that revolution the means have been named by Stalin in his *Questions of Leninism:* "Any dodge, trick, ruse, cunning, unlawful method, concealment, the veiling of truth. The basic rule is to exploit . . . to dodge, to maneuver." That is to say, since there is no God, there is no law, no truth, no justice, no right or wrong. When God goes everything goes.

Perhaps, after all, Atheistic Communism has done the world a favor. We did not know because we did not see. Now we see and we know.

Chapter 10

"Where Now Is Thy God?"

THE question, "Where Now Is Thy God?" was first asked of the Jews by idolatrous heathen. It indicated an exceedingly primitive mentality. The heathen said in effect: We have gods that can be seen. The God of Israel cannot be seen. Where *is* your God? Again and again that taunt was flung at the Hebrews by Philistines, Moabites, Assyrians, Babylonians, and the half dozen other idolatrous peoples who surrounded them, hemmed them in, threatened them, fought them, persecuted, exiled them, but worst of all, tempted them to abandon the invisible Jehovah and accept Moloch, Baal, Isis, Osiris, Merodach.

But the answer to the heathen came swift and sure from the mouth of those who had learned the Law. "God cannot be seen by mortal eyes. No man hath seen God at any time. God is no stick or stone. God is no image of baked clay. You cannot pick up a handful of mud out of the bed of the Nile or the Tigris or the Jordan, fashion it with your hands, put it in a kiln like any piece of pottery and bring it out a god. Your gods—your heathen gods—are the work of the hands of man; they are not God at all. Man does not make God. God makes man."

Those early Jews had learned in the synagogue what Moses had taught from Mount Sinai, and what the prophets had retold in phrases ever varying but ever the same, sometimes in solemn majestic utterance, sometimes in familiar speech more adapted to the mental level and the taste of simple people. In Isaias we find this magnificent passage: "To whom then have you likened God?

64

or what image will you make for him? Hath the workman cast
a graven *statue?* or hath the goldsmith formed it with gold, or
the silversmith with plates of silver . . . Do you not know? hath
it not been heard? hath it not been with you from the beginning?
have you not understood the foundations of the earth? It is he that
sitteth upon the globe of the earth . . . he that stretcheth out the
heavens as nothing, and spreadeth them as a tent to dwell in.
He that bringeth the searchers of secrets to nothing, that hath
made the judges of the earth as vanity . . . To whom have ye
likened me, or made me equal, saith the Holy One? Lift up your
eyes on high, and see who hath created these things . . . Knowest
thou not, or hast thou not heard? the Lord is the everlasting
God, who hath created the ends of the earth: he shall not faint,
nor labour, neither is there any searching out of his wisdom."

There are a dozen passages like that in Isaias, and the temptation is to continue with his superb descriptions of the One True
God. But Isaias was a versatile and resourceful orator. He did not
always speak in stately measures. A master of many methods he
switches suddenly from the majestic dignity of a Demosthenes
or a Cicero to the caustic irony of a Tertullian or a Savonarola,
as he ridicules the manufactured gods of the heathen:

"The smith hath wrought with his file, with coals, and with
hammers he hath formed it. . . . The carpenter hath stretched out
his rule, he hath formed it with a plane: he hath made it with
corners, and hath fashioned it round with the compass: and he
hath made the image of a man as it were a beautiful man dwelling
in a house. He hath cut down cedars, taken the holm, and the
oak that stood among the trees of the forest: he hath planted
the pine tree, which the rain hath nourished. And it hath served
men for fuel: he took thereof, and warmed himself: and he
kindled it, and baked bread: but of the rest he made a god, and
adored it: he made a graven thing, and bowed down before it.
Part of it he burnt with fire, and with part of it he dressed his
meat . . . But the residue thereof he made a god, and a graven

thing for himself: he boweth down before it, and adoreth it, and prayeth unto it, saying: Deliver me, for thou art my God."

It is a curious fact—curious and pathetic—that seven hundred years later the apostle Paul was obliged to tell the sophisticated Athenians what Isaias had told the primitive barbaric heathen: "God, who made the world, and all things therein; he, being Lord of heaven and earth, dwelleth not in temples made with hands; neither is he served with men's hands, as though he needed any thing; seeing it is he who giveth to all life, and breath, and all things: . . . For in him we live, and move. . . . Being therefore the offspring of God, we must not suppose the divinity to be like unto gold, or silver, or stone, the graving of art, and device of man."

Stranger still, some four hundred years after St. Paul, we find St. Augustine, (in his youth influenced by the Manichees who had brought to Italy and North Africa the superstitions of Persia), confessing bitterly that for a time he did not know how to conceive of God: "Knowing not the true Being, I was so shaken by quips and quiddities that I had no answer for these silly deceivers when they asked me what is the origin of evil? whether God is limited by a bodily form? . . . My eye could see nothing but bodies, and my mind nothing but materialized ideas. I did not understand that God is a spirit, who has no parts that can be measured, whose being is not a bulk, because bulk . . . cannot be wholly everywhere like God, who is spirit. And I had not the least conception in what we are like God, or whether Scripture was right in saying that we are in the image of God."

And again: "I marshalled before the sight of my spirit all creation, all that we see, earth, and sea, and air, and stars, and trees, and animals; all that we do not see, the firmament of the sky above, and all angels, and all spiritual things for these also, as if they were bodies, did my imagination arrange in this place or in that. I pictured to myself Thy creation as one vast mass, composed of various kinds of bodies, some real bodies, some those which I imagined in place of spirits . . . And Thee, O Lord, I conceived as lapping it round and interpenetrating it everywhere, but as infinite in every direction; as if there were sea everywhere, and everywhere through measureless space nothing but illimitable sea, and within this sea a sponge, huge but yet finite; the sponge would be pervaded through all its particles by the infinite sea . . . And I said to myself, 'Behold God, behold God's creation.'"

Now it may be a fancy of mine, but I seem to find in the passage—"Not knowing the True Being, I was shaken by quips and quiddities"—a prophecy of some very highly educated pagans of our own day. Fifteen hundred years after St. Augustine, certain doctors of science, having rejected the True God, substitute in His place "quips and quiddities." They have invented a hundred gods—gods of the laboratory, gods of the test tube, gods of chemical combinations; gods of physical force; the dynamo god of Eugene O'Neill's strange terrible play, fantastic imaginative things that do not exist, the Life Force god of Bernard Shaw, the *élan-vital* god, the Creative Evolution god of Bergson, Time-Space, the hyphenated god (most unintelligible of all). Men even make god of an abstraction like Auguste Comte's Humanity (with a capital H) and I don't know whether that be not a cruder superstition than the gods of the heathen fashioned of wood or stone or brass. After all, wood and stone and brass are something, and an abstraction is nothing.

A generation ago laboratory workers were breaking up the molecule; today they are smashing the atom, looking—whether they know it or not—for God. "I have examined many systems purporting to be atheistic," said James Clark Maxwell, premier physicist of a generation ago, "but I have always found in them a God concealed somewhere."

Yes, there is a God hidden away in the laboratory amongst the Bunsen burners and the test tubes, out of sight beneath the atoms, the ions, the electrons. "Raise the stone and thou shalt find Me. Cleave the wood and there am I," says God, the same

God who said "Seek and ye shall find." But the pathetic fact about science is that so many scientists, with God under their eyes, do not see Him; with God at the tips of their fingers, do not touch Him. "O Father," said our Lord, "Thou hast hidden these things from the wise and prudent and hast revealed them to the little ones . . . Blessed are the eyes that see what you see." "God," says the mystic Eckhart, "is nearer to me than I am to myself: He is just as near to wood and stone, but they do not know it." "They do not know it": the saddest words of tongue or pen. "He was in the world, and the world was made by Him, and the world knew Him not." If you ask these pitiable scientific folk "Where now is thy God?," they say, sometimes with scorn but again with wistfulness, "We do not even know if there be a God." If a man without a country is an object of commiseration, if a Melchisedech "without father, without mother, without descent" is a lonely figure in the world of the sons of men and women, what shall we say of the man who in answer to the question "Where is thy God?" says, "I know not." "Great God, I'd rather be a pagan suckled in a creed outworn" than that most forlorn object in all creation, the man who knows not whence he came or whither he goes, because he has caught no glimpse of God, the Alpha and Omega, the Beginning and the End.

But there are those who, after much mental labor, spiritual anguish, and moral struggle, have won their way through "like the Catholic man who hath mightily won God out of knowledge and good out of pain, sight out of blindness and purity out of stain," as Sidney Lanier says. And perhaps of all men in any generation who have mightily won God out of knowledge and good out of pain, the most conspicuous and the most articulate was St. Augustine. This most learned of the Fathers of the Church, east or west, was no stranger to books. He spent his life with books and he wrote a whole library. But seeking God he did not confine himself to pages of print. Unlike the alchemists of his day (sometimes I wonder if they were really more foolish

or superstitious than materialists of our day) he did not lock
himself in a laboratory with fire and bellows and copper retorts
to wrest from the chemical elements and physical forces the secret
of being and of motion. Hundreds of years before our American
poet, he had followed the injunction, "Go forth under the open
sky and list to Nature's teachings." He interrogated Nature and
Nature replied to him. Nature does speak if we ask reverently
and await her answer in silence. "I asked the earth and it said
'I am not He.' I asked the sea and the depths and the creeping
things that have life and they answered, 'We are not Thy God,
look above us.' I asked the breezes and the gales, and the whole
air with its inhabitants said to me 'Anaximenes is in error, I am
not God.' I asked the heaven, the sun, the moon and the stars.
'We too,' said they, 'are not the God Whom thou seekest.' And
I said to all the creatures that surrounded the doors of my fleshy
senses, 'Ye have said to me of my God that ye are not He: tell
me somewhat of Him.' And with a great voice they exclaimed
'It is He that hath made us.'"

But why is it that if nature speaks to St. Augustine she does
not give an answer, that same answer, to all who ask her? Some
people look upon the sun and moon and stars and see no sign of
God. Others—poets, saints, mystics—lose themselves in an ecstasy
because they see God in a landscape, a cloud, a lightning flash, a
wave breaking upon the shore. A sunset to them is a glimpse of
the heavenly Jerusalem; a path of light from the moon upon the
waters shows the way into another and lovelier world. Even
philosophers, an unimpressionable breed, have confessed that the
sight of the starry heavens filled them with awe. But to some—
to not a few in our own skeptical generation—the sea and the sun
and the stars speak, if they speak at all, in vain. Why?

St. Paul, who perhaps is somewhat more abrupt in his speech
than St. Augustine, seems to say that all men should know God
from His creation. "The invisible things of Him, from the creation
of the world, are clearly seen, being understood by the things that

are made; His eternal power also, and divinity; so that they are inexcusable. . . . Professing themselves to be wise, they became fools."

"Inexcusable" is a strong word. "Fools" is a stronger word. In regard to those who cannot see God in creation, St. Augustine is, a little more lenient. He says that religious belief is not capable of proof, at least to all men. But perhaps we have a solution of the apparent contradiction of two great saints in the words of our Savior Himself. "Blessed are the clean of heart: for they shall see God." A clean heart is one in which there is no impurity. We often speak of the sin of the flesh as if it were only one kind of sin. But St. Paul has a long catalogue of sins of the flesh. "The works of the flesh," he says, "are manifest, which are fornication, uncleanness, immodesty, luxury, idolatry, witchcrafts, enmities, contentions, emulation, wraths, quarrels, dissensions, sects, envies, murders, drunkenness, revellings, and such like. Of the which I foretell you, as I have foretold to you, that they who do such things shall not obtain the kingdom of God."

They shall not obtain the kingdom of God. They shall not so much as see God. We see objects in nature with the eyes of our head. A murderer, a lecher, an ambitious, selfish, cruel or covetous person can, I dare say, see a sunrise or a mountain or a waterfall quite as well as the pure in heart. But there are the eyes of the mind and soul as well as eyes of flesh. We see God not with these eyes fixed in a socket in the skull, but with the eyes of the spirit. These eyes of the spirit are dimmed or blinded not only by adulteries, but by contentions, emulations, wraths, quarrels, envies, revellings, and the rest. The pure of heart are those who have driven not some but all of these vices out of their heart.

And there, I believe, is the answer to the question that is in the minds of many: "I have no difficulty in seeing God in Beauty. But Nature is not only beauty; Nature is in some of its aspects ugly, vile, horrible. You speak of sunsets but what of earthquakes,

cyclones, hurricanes, mass slaughter, all those calamities which
the civil law calls 'An act of God.' How can I see God in pestilence, famine, drouth, in a conflagration started by lightning;
how can I see God in tuberculosis, in carcinoma, in such a plague
as syphilis which afflicts the innocent no less than the guilty? If
wars, with all their attendant and consequent horrors, are to be
laid at the door of willful man, is God responsible for pestilence
and plague and all the other hideous manifestations of pitiless
nature?"

In reply to such a heart-rending protestation as that what
can any one say? No man can solve the everlasting problem of
evil. But perhaps one may ask the questioner if he has entirely
purified his heart of all obstacles to spiritual sight.

Perhaps it would be well to read again the book of Job, that
unequaled blending of profound philosophy and lofty poetry.
The author of that book, like a composer of sublime music, takes
as his theme that very question, "Where Now Is Thy God?,"
and plays upon it like Beethoven or Brahms in a superb sym-
phony. It is the most poignant, penetrating, eloquent drama of
the problem that tortures us all. Let us pray that we may conclude
with that ancient sufferer, "Although [God] should kill me, I
will trust in him."

One thing more may be said. We can look upon the Cross
of Christ. He surely had done no harm. If no other man was
innocent Jesus was innocent. He was the loveliest of all the
children of men. Yet there He hangs in agony, a supreme example
to all the innocent who suffer. All who love God are on that
Cross with Christ. "With Christ I am nailed to the cross," says
St. Paul. The innocent Christian like the innocent Christ, agonizes
upon the Cross that those who are not innocent may be saved.
If one needs not expiation for his own sins, he may offer his
sufferings to God in union with Him who needed not expiation
for sin because there was no sin in Him. "Suffering," says one
writer on the Mystic Life, "plunges like a sword through creation,

leaving on the one side cringing and degraded animals and on the other side heroes and saints." If we look upon the Cross and learn the Gospel of the Cross we shall be not cringing and degraded, not even plaintive but heroic and saintly. Those who have absorbed the lesson of the Cross, when asked "Where now is thy God?" point to Jesus bleeding, agonizing, about to give up the ghost, and they say, "*There* is my God."

PART IV

JESUS CHRIST
AND HIS CHURCH

Chapter 11

The Christ They Do Not See

In ANOTHER chapter we shall consider the perhaps debatable thesis that we do not see with our eyes, or even with the uninhibited mind. We see with our predispositions, prejudices, passions. We see with inherited tendencies and hidden antipathies. If to "see" is to perceive, lay hold of, grasp, appreciate, there is always danger that when we look at a person, an institution, a government, a nation, a race, people other than our own, we do not see it in a clear atmosphere but through a "smog." If the object under inspection is controversial (is there anything worthwhile that is not "controversial"?), we apprehend it quite as much with the unconscious as with the conscious mind. One highly "controversial" phenomenon is the Catholic Church. We shall come to that now. I offer an even more important fact: It is difficult for a hostile or even neutral mind to "see" Jesus Christ.

When the Divine Child was presented by His mother in the Temple, the holy man Simeon acting as a prophet (on that occasion only) said: "This Child is set for the fall and for the resurrection of many in Israel, and *for a sign* that *shall be contradicted.*" That prophecy, which strikes so jarring a note in St. Luke's idyllic story of the Infancy, was quickly verified. Jesus had to be hurried away out of the reach of Herod. Later when He returned and entered upon His mission, He became and He remained—indeed He remains to this day—a center of controversy. The question "What think you of Christ?" is still asked and is answered in a great variety of ways. After all these centuries even those who believe in Him (in one way or other), not to say those who do not believe, cannot agree upon what manner of man He was—and is. When He came the entire world had been expecting Him since Moses, since Abraham, since Adam. But the world didn't recognize Him. "He was in the world and the world was made by Him and the world knew Him not. He came unto His own and His own received Him not."

The poor peasants of Palestine were inclined to take Him at His own valuation, but they were too frightened to confess their faith. Poor people under the rule of tyrants do not dare speak their mind. Fear, like hate, can be blinding. In Galilee it was generally admitted that Jesus spoke as no man had ever spoken before. Also He worked wonders. But the authorities, civil and ecclesiastical, were against Him, and it was therefore both treason and heresy to see the Messias in Jesus.

One poor fellow indeed, the man born blind, to whom Jesus had given sight, was emboldened to "talk back" to the officials. The repartee is unique in the Gospels: "How did He open thy eyes?" "I have told you already and you have heard; why would you hear it again; will you also become his disicples?" "Be *thou* his diciples! *We* are the disciples of Moses. As to this man we know not from whence he is." "Why, herein is a wonderful thing, that you know not from whence he is and he hath opened my eyes."

It is always so with skeptics when a preternatural phenomenon occurs. They first of all refuse to acknowledge it; they go off into a digression and start an argument. In the case of the man born blind the proper procedure would have been to verify the fact, interrogate the witnesses and ask an explanation of the One who was alleged to have performed the miracle. Instead of following that reasonable, and as we say nowadays "scientific" course of action, the unbelievers browbeat the man, ignored the witnesses and cast slurs upon Jesus.

In our day the procedure is not essentially different. David Hume said that no evidence however overwhelming could prove a miracle because "miracles do not happen." That dogma is accepted as definitive by modern skeptics. Confronted with what purports to be a miracle, they scoff at the suggestion of medical or surgical investigation, denounce the witnesses as superstitious and dismiss the case with some such phrase as "the laws of nature are inviolable." On one occasion—one of many—I happened to speak to a physican about Lourdes, and in particular about Dr. Alexis Carrel's account of what he saw there. My friend the doctor said simply, "I do not accept the supernatural." And that was that. The good man did not realize that in this case the believer was "scientific" and the unbeliever "dogmatic."

The hostile critics who investigated Jesus could not "see" Him because of their mental predispositions. I can imagine one such agent, sent from Jerusalem to Galilee to spy upon Jesus, in a dialogue at the Sanhedrin:

"Well," says the High Priest, "what have you to report?"

"The trip was a waste of time," he answers. "The fellow is a peasant, not a gentleman, not a scholar. He is an ignoramus; he teaches without having learned. He has had no course in rabbinical theology. He has sat at the feet of neither Hillel nor Shammai. He roams over the countryside telling little stories to simple people about a Samaritan who is a better man than priest or levite; about a scapegrace son who demands his inheritance, wastes it on harlots and yet is received back by his father with affection and honor. He doesn't say it in so many words but he gives the people to understand that God is like the father of the profligate.

"I have it on the best authority, a rich Pharisee named Simon, that a shameless woman, one that should by law have been stoned, actually burst into Simon's house, threw herself down before this charlatan and spilled upon his feet a vase of costly ointment. Instead of expressing wrath at this indecency and extravagance, he had the effrontery to praise the woman and to rebuke Simon at his own table.

"He goes about accompanied by a motley mob. He has no dignity and no sense of propriety. His associates are by preference of the lower class. You have only to look at them to see that they are the makings of criminals and disturbers of the peace.

"I took the pains to look up his background. He was born in—of all places—a stable, a kind of grotto, a mere hole in the rock. There was something irregular about his parentage. On that point my informants in Galilee were not too positive, for it seems that he was born away from home. Obviously there was something to conceal, or his parents would not have taken pains to escape observation on the occasion of his birth.

"But the people—ignorant and uncouth as always—seem to care nothing about these shameful facts. They run after him in great swarms. On one occasion I estimated three thousand and again five thousand crowding around him. He has cast a spell over them. But these Galileans, as you know, are, like the Samaritans, half heathen. How could they be expected to know a true prophet from a false?

"Miracles? Signs and wonders? I saw none. There was a great deal of babble about such things. But you know how the people are: fond of legends and myths. Even if this man does some magic, it must be by Satan not by Jehovah.

"Did I hear on any occasion a voice out of the clouds? Did I see this Jesus on a mountain transfigured by a light from heaven? Nonsense! There was no voice. There was no light from heaven."

"But what is this disturber up to?"

"I don't know. But I did hear him on one occasion make a contrast between God and Caesar. I take it he was advising the people not to give tribute to the Romans. Come to think of it, there we have him. We can hale this Jesus before the Procurator and accuse him of disloyalty to the Emperor. The political angle is always good. Let Pilate attend to the matter. If the Roman hesitates,

we can accuse him also of disloyalty. There, I think, gentlemen
of the Sanhedrin, we come to the conclusion of our investigation
and the solution of the problem. Let us accuse this disturber of
disloyalty to the State."

I will not insult readers of this imagined dialogue by applying
the moral. Suffice to say, that's how they looked at Jesus, that's
what they saw.

There are, however, two or three points of resemblance between the case of the Church and that of her Founder. On the
day these lines are written I have read in an English paper words
of the Archbishop of Canterbury, spoken on the occasion of
his announcing the coming of delegates from the Orthodox
Church in Russia to confer with Anglican prelates in London:
"The greatest existing hindrance to the advance of the kingdom
of God among men is the Roman Catholic Church." Our
"brother in Christ" and with him a considerable number of men
in high ecclesiastical position in England and America think
Catholicism a greater menace than Russian or international Communism. They look at us, and that is what they see.

A journalist of the Archbishop's own communion and in his
own See called the Anglican primate's statement "fantastic." We
could think of a shorter and uglier word, but we Catholics have
learned by centuries of experience that no opinion about us, no
judgment upon us is too cruel or too absurd to be spoken. The
disciple is not above the Master. The Church is not more sacrosanct than her creator. "They did such things in the green wood,
what will they do in the dry?"

Another application of the story of the spy who looked at Christ
and could not see Him may be made in the case of the Church.
What I have called "the political angle" suffices in the one case
and the other. From the days of the Roman Empire all critics
of the Church—Elizabethan and Cromwellian in England, Robespierre and the *Directoire* in France, Bismark and Hitler in Germany, Garibaldi and Mazzini in Italy, Calles in Mexico, Peron

in the Argentine, and a long line of super "patriots" in the United States—have taken pains to explain that they do not oppose us on grounds of religion, but because we are a political menace.

It's an ancient device but it still does yeoman service. Demagogues and dictators in all ages have made use of it, but it is also effective in a democracy where the people are supposed to think for themselves. It would be more honorable if our critics would attack us upon the ground of philosophy and theology. It is demagogic to raise the cry "unpatriotic." It reminds us of Dr. Johnson's definition: "the last refuge of a scoundrel."

But the opposition must not think that they deceive us. Nor, we think, do they deceive our fellow citizens.

Chapter 12

Christ and the People

It is difficult to understand why Christ the Lord, the greatest glory of our race, was not generally recognized as such while he was on earth. After all these years and at this distance we see Him for what He was and is. Even those who have no religious faith vie with us in pouring out upon our Savior such encomiums as are spoken of no other person in history. Ernest Renan who labored at the ungracious task of destroying the orthodox view of Jesus, wrote towards the close of his work *Vie de Jésus* a panegyric that negates all that he had said by way of denigration: "Rest now in thy glory, noble initiator. Thy work is completed; thy divinity is established. Henceforth thou shalt be present, from the heights of thy divine peace, in the infinite consequences for thy acts . . . For thousands of years the world will extol thee. Banner of our contradictions, thou wilt be the sign around which will be fought the fiercest battles. A thousand times more living, a thousand times more loved since thy death than during the days of thy pilgrimage here below, thou wilt become to such a degree the corner-stone of humanity, that to tear thy name from this world would be to shake it to its foundations. Between thee and God, men will no longer distinguish. Complete conqueror of death, take possession of thy kingdom, whither, by the royal road thou has traced, ages of adorers will follow thee."

Renan had started out to "cut" Jesus "down to size." In attempting to do so, he said many things insulting and even blasphemous, but in the end, like Julian the Apostate, he was compelled to cry "Thou hast conquered, Galilean."

It is not my present purpose however to cite examples of admiration and of worship spoken of and to Jesus. To do so would require an anthology of encyclopedic size. Not all the books in the world, says St. John, could contain the things which Jesus did. And, we may add, not all the books written about all other historic persons could equal in number or in enthusiasm what has been written in praise of Jesus Christ.

Why then did Jesus receive such slender recognition when He appeared among men? "He was in the world and the world was made by him," says St. John, "but the world knew Him not: He came unto His own and His own received Him not." But why! What was wrong with His generation and His people that they could not recognize their Savior? It may be it was from pondering over that problem, quite as much as because of Divine Revelation, that Cardinal Newman was led to speak of "some aboriginal calamity that set man against his Maker." Be that as it may, the fact is Jesus very soon came to know He was unwelcome. Everyone was against Him, Pharisees, Sadducees, Herodians, Jews, Romans and at the end all but a handful of the simple people who had for the moment been inclined to acclaim Him Messiah.

Preachers of the Passion make a telling point of the fact that Pharisees and Sadducees, normally at odds, composed their differences, and that Pilate and Herod forgot their feud in mutual antagonism to the inoffensive Galilean. But few preachers go on to ask and answer the question, "Why?" What was there about Jesus that brought His enemies together not in love of one another but in hatred of Him? What was there about Him that made Him the most "controversial character" (to borrow a modern expression) that ever appeared among men? Putting aside the supernatural reason "it behooveth that one man should die for the people," what was there in the life and teaching of Jesus that annoyed men, embittered and alienated them? To narrow the theme, I suggest that we omit, at least from this chapter, consideration of the more responsible villains in the piece—Pharisees, Scribes, Sadducees, Pilate, Herod—and ask why the people, having at first taken Jesus to their heart turned against Him.

I am inclined to think that the proximate cause was the fact that Christ would neither conform nor compromise. He could have "saved his skin," as men say, with what is called prudence. But He would have none of it. The keynote to His preaching was His own admonition, "Let your yea be yea and your nay nay." Ambiguity, duplicity, purposeful obscurity are for diplomats and politicians not for prophets—not for the Savior. Those who seek what they themselves cynically call "the will of the people" expressed by ballot, or by a show of hands, or *viva voce,* consider Christ's method fatal. They favor the technique of Mark Antony speaking to the mob over the dead body of Caesar: flattery, cajolery, deceit, appeal to hatred and vengeance. Modern examples of that method may be found in the pages of the newspapers almost any day. Few professional politicians consider their constituents entitled to the truth. Indeed it is not rare that top ranking "statesmen" practise deception upon the people at large and even the members of their own party. In the rash of "Memoirs" that broke out after the Second World War there was evidence that some of those in the top echelons of our national government hid the truth, if they did not actually lie—even to one another. How then could the common people expect better treatment than their superiors?

Now it is true that Jesus said on one occasion to His immediate disciples, "I have many things to say to you, but you cannot bear them now," and He did postpone letting the general throng know just what He claimed to be and what He had in mind. But whatever degree of reserve He preached was from pity not from scorn. When the proper time arrived He spoke out, though He knew that He would lose great numbers of adherents by doing so. Our Savior was not indifferent to the goodwill of the people. But He refused to adapt His Gospel to their expectations, still less to their prejudices and passions. He was, as a matter of fact, a popular hero for a year or more and He could have remained so. The formula was simple—a call to resistance perhaps to arms against the Romans. That was what kept the Pharisees in power and in favor. "Pharisee" means "Separatist." The Herodians favored what we have come to call "peaceful coexistence," but the Pharisees were behind—discreetly and sometimes secretly behind—every incipient rebellion against the pagans who had come in upon the Jews and had made them in effect a nation of slaves. Jesus was no such "patriot." In fact He would be called in this modern age a "pacifist." If the favor of the people had been His primary objective, He went the wrong way about it. There was something of a parallel in Ireland shortly before the Emancipation in 1829. Daniel O'Connell at the height of his popularity declared that the freedom of Ireland was not worth the shedding of one drop of Irish blood. It is a wonder that he did not at that moment lose his following, the entire nation. There is probably no greater instance of moral courage in the life of any "friend of the people" in the political world. When a race of men is eager for rebellion—perhaps even justified rebellion—and on the *qui vive* for the cry "To arms," the hero who refuses point blank to speak that word may lose in that one moment his reputation as hero and be dubbed traitor.

Something of this may have been in Lord Acton's mind when he said "All power corrupts: absolute power corrupts absolutely"; and in the mind also of the one who said, "All great men are bad." At a crucial moment—at what he himself may prefer to call the climactic moment—he is tempted to cry "To arms!" Resistance to that temptation is the greatest of all acts of magnanimity.

It has been said that we Americans were not led but were lied into the Second World War. If deception and self-contradiction are equivalent to lying, we were also lied into the First World War. If a third such war occurs, it will come because the people —our own included—will have become bewildered by double-dealing and double-talking leaders. "Tell the truth," says Christ.

Telling the truth would be disastrous, say the diplomats. The yea yea, nay nay policy would never do in international negotiation. Duplicity has been employed ever since Machiavelli, and doubtless before him. Christ's method has been rejected. Hence have we wars.

The people make heroes to their own image and likeness or rather to their own pattern of greatness. It matters not to them whether or not a man possesses moral integrity. If he has power and uses it, as they think, to their advantage, they exalt Alexander, Xerxes, Antiochus, Caesar, Pompey, Augustus, Napoleon, Hitler, Mussolini, Peron, every one immoral. In Russia on Lenin's birthday a million poor people take their place in line, file into the sepulchre and, to all intents and purposes, adore the devil as a deity.

In our country it would not be difficult to name certain men who, as the phrase goes, have "achieved eminence" in political life, and have "made a place for themselves in the hearts of the people." Many of them were tricksters, political charlatans; some of them—not a few—actually wicked. By some strange and as it were suicidal tendency, the people have loved and admired and rewarded those who did them harm.

If Jesus Christ could *per impossible* have been unprincipled enough to play upon the passions and the weaknesses of the people He could have won and held their allegiance. But He would not deceive them and He would not permit them to deceive themselves. So the people *en masse* deserted Him. He was a disappointment to them. "We *had* hoped," they said, "that it *might* have been He that was to redeem Israel." No more disconsolate sentence was ever spoken. So it came to pass that there never was in all history a great man who had so few friends about him when He came to die. What happened after His death and ever since is the greatest of all evidences that ultimately Good will prevail even here below. Leaders of men generally have no patience with that word "ultimately." They would be idolized, here, now, while they are alive to enjoy their fame. It was otherwise with Jesus Christ.

As with the people, so with the two other groups, (let us call them after our modern fashion), Church and State, Our Lord was equally uncompromising. They were the upper and nether millstone between which Our Lord was to be crushed. If He had been willing to act shrewdly (or as men say prudently) He could have maneuvered so as to pit each of those formidable adversaries against the other and escape from both when they came into conflict. Many demagogues and dictators have played that game. But there was no shrewdness in the character of Christ. In that He was different from St. Paul. When the great apostle was mobbed and on the point of being murdered on the steps of the castle of Lysias he resorted to a piece of adroit strategy and, for the time being, escaped. Our Savior of course was not a Roman citizen, but if He had been it is doubtful that He would in any circumstance have claimed His right to a Roman trial. He remained on the ground, met the Pharisees face to face and time and again excoriated them with such invective as is not found in Cicero's diatribes against Catiline or in the Philippics of Demosthenes. There is a phrase applied to Tertullian, "the perfervid African," but there is no more severe denunciation in Tertullian than in the twenty-third chapter of St. Matthew. Sentimental readers of the Bible who seem to remember nothing of the Old Testament except the 23d Psalm and nothing of the New Testament but the Sermon on the Mount, have fashioned for themselves a false image of religion. If Our Lord had been the kind of Person they imagine He might have escaped crucifixion. But to judge from His utter recklessness or, if that be considered too violent a word, His refusal to placate His enemies, He would have thought it ignoble to compromise or temporize with evil. Perhaps it is disregard of the element of vigor in the character of Christ that prevents our civilization from being Christian.

Chapter 13

Christ and the Philosophers

CHRIST has sometimes been called "the Jewish Socrates." For those who take Socrates to be the wisest of men and one of the noblest, the tribute is superlative, but to the Christian the comparison is, however well intended, uncomplimentary. Socrates was noble and good judged by standards that prevailed in the heathen world before Christ. But the Son of God introduced to the race a new concept of man. Since His time the ideal has been Himself. Towards that ideal Christians can approximate more easily than pre-Christians. Or, we may add, post-Christians. Thousands of holy souls in and out of the calendar of saints came nearer to the Christ ideal than Socrates. In fact if we were to compare Socrates with Christ we should find, with Dean Farrar in *The Life of Lives,* that the best of pagans make a sorry figure beside Jesus.

Even if we evaluate Christ and Socrates not in the moral or spiritual order but in the matter of pedagogical method, the difference remains incalculable. Socrates was first and last a seeker after knowledge. He made his way step by step from the known to the unknown. With Jesus there was no need of a reasoning process. He came to knowledge as a prophet does, by intuition and contemplation, not by laborious and hazardous ratiocination. To know all Truth He had only to look within and above. "Look in thine own heart" is a wise rule for any one who wishes to know. Man is all the world in small compass. But when Jesus looked within He saw more than man. "The Father and I," He said, "are one."

The people noticed the difference between the One who knew because He knew, who knew because He was what He was, and over against Him those who learned by studying. "This man speaks as one having authority and not as the Scribes and Pharisees." Jesus sometimes said "Behold I tell you the truth." But He went far beyond that with the proclamation—in anyone but Him blasphemous—I *am* the Truth.

Socrates made no such claim. In *Phaedo* he speaks after this fashion: "If what I say is true then I do well to be persuaded of the truth." Again: "This is my state of mind in which I approach the argument," implying that his state of mind might change. Again: "Whereas he [the non-philosopher] seeks to convince his hearers that what he says is true, I am rather trying to convince myself." And—now herein we have the key to the Socratic method—"I would ask you to be thinking of the truth and not of Socrates; therefore, agree with me if I seem to you to be speaking the truth, or if not, withstand me might and main, that I may not deceive you as well as myself."

All this is the antithesis of the manner and method of Jesus. One of His favorite expressions was "It hath been said to you of old [such and such] but *I* say to you." He made no explanation, no apologies. He did not amend or modify what He had said. He confessed no uncertainty about His doctrine. Nor did He condescend on any occasion to justify Himself. To the challenge "By what authority," He replied with a question which threw the quesioners off balance and silenced them. He did not recur to the question "By what authority." His authority was Himself. His Gospel was Himself.

The difference between Jesus and Socrates, the prophet and the philosopher, has a parallel in our day. The Church, to which Jesus said: "As the living Father has sent Me, so I send you; the works that I have done you also shall do; go teach, go preach—I am with you all days"; the Church, I say, speaks as One having authority and not as those who at best make "guesses at the riddle of existence." The Church speaks not with hesitation and trepidation, but confidently, forthrightly and as Jesus did, dogmatically. She does not feel her way along, stumbling foward a little, retracing her steps, teaching one doctrine today but reversing her view tomorrow. She speaks absolutely and apodictically like the One who created her and sent her forth to preach and to teach.

The vocation of the Church in other words, is that of the prophet, not the philosopher. She does not despise philosophy. She has a philosophy of her own. That philosophy may, like any other, take on certain characteristics of the thought of the day. Once it was predominantly Platonic; it has retained a great deal of Plato (and hence of Socrates) but later became more largely Aristotelian. In due time the Church's philosophy will absorb whatever seems good to her in one or more of the philosophies of our day. But she will exercise the right to eliminate from what she takes any elements which she recognizes as inconsistent with her Gospel. After all, the Gospel is revealed and philosophy—any philosophy—is only contrived. The Gospel is everlasting; philosophy transient, changeable, evanescent. The Gospel is of God; philosophy is of man.

In our day as in all days since Socrates, professors of philosophy play with ideas, take up a system of thought and drop it, take up another and another and so spend a lifetime in the search for truth. But it is the primary tenet of all their systems that truth is not really discoverable or permanently tenable. Man can never know whether what he holds today will seem, or be, true tomorrow. He may stumble upon truth and not recognize it. He picks up truth and lets it drop, not even aware that he held it for a moment.

"What is truth?" asked Pilate. The typical modern answer is that truth is a will-o-the-wisp. Through the bogs and marshes you pursue it but it evades capture. What is truth? A drop of mercury which when you put your finger upon it is not there. What is truth? It is a state of mind. What is true for you may be false for me. What I take to be truth may seem illusion, or prejudice or superstition to you. Your truth is yours and my truth is mine.

So the search for truth is unending. It is a race which can never be won. St. Paul's statement "I run not as at an uncertainty" but so as to reach the goal and obtain the prize, does not apply, they say, in the race for philosophical truth. In that race there is no starting point, no markers along the course to indicate progress, no goal, no prize—no prize except the exhilaration incidental to effort. Such a concept as that, Christ would have considered blasphemous. "For this was I born," He said, "and for this am I come into the world, that I should give testimony to the truth." "You shall know the truth and the truth will make you free," free from the torture of everlasting searching without hope of finding.

Oddly enough there are religious bodies bearing Christ's name which hold to the philosophers' view that truth can never be certainly known and securely held. They are aware that other religious bodies, also under the name of Christ, hold views of truth different from their own. They say the other man's truth is true for him, as their own is true for them. There are many truths and therefore no sure truth. The best we can hope is an approximation to the truth.

Nor can the heart resolve the perplexity of the mind. The other man is as devout and as docile to the Spirit as I. How then shall I claim that wherein he differs from me, he is mistaken? We shall have to go on, he and I, that other Church and mine, without ever being sure that what we believe is *The* Truth. Such a conclusion may be philosophy, but it is not religion—not religion but agnosticism.

Time and again in shops where books on religion are sold one comes upon a new volume with some such title as *Reappraisal of Religious Faith*. It would seem that there is always need of a reappraisal, and in due time a reappraisal of the reappraisal. What our grandfathers believed, we are told, is now incredible and intolerable. What we believe—our type of Christian faith—will appear impossible to our descendants. At no stage in the process of reappraisal will it be possible to say: "This is final; this shall last until the end of time."

In other words there are those to whom Christian religion is only a philosophy, variable with the ages and with the temperament of the believer. The alternative is belief in a Church that teaches with the authority of Christ, that is to say infallibly.

Chapter 14

Seeing Christ: Seeing the Church

IN CONTRAST with the hostile emissaries from Jerusalem who came to spy upon Jesus, there were well-disposed observers in Samaria and Galilee. They were mostly poor people and, by the standard of the intellectuals of that day, ignorant. They had, in fact, little schooling but they had a spiritual discernment often lacking in the learned. They recognized a purer religion in the parables of Jesus than in the suffocating casuistry and the crushing traditions of the Elders.

Later on, among the Gentiles, St. Paul was to discover the same curious fact: spiritual vision and intellectual pretension are seldom found together. Jesus had little success among the learned in Jerusalem; St. Paul received his worst set-back in Athens. The Sanhedrin and the Academy were equally slow to recognize truth in the spiritual order. In the modern world those who have been, and remain even yet, hoodwinked by Communism are the "liberals" and the "intelligentsia." "Not many wise," said St. Paul, were among the early Christians and the same remains true today.

"This accursed people," said the Pharisees, "knoweth not the law." Perhaps not, and if not it may have been just as well that they did not. The "law" was simple enough but when lawyers everywhere and always speak of the "law" they include mountainous commentaries upon the law. Jesus said: "Woe to you lawyers; you bind impossible burdens upon the backs of the poor." Incidentally, it was for utterances such as those that the objects of the scorn of Christ silenced Him. But ignorant or not, the simple people could recognize a prophet when they saw Him. It did not scandalize them that a great teacher should come from their own ranks. They did not ask, "Can any good come out of Nazareth?" The prophets had not all been of the priestly caste or of the nobility. The woman at the well in Samaria, heathen and sinner as she was, promptly said when Jesus had read her soul, "Sir, I perceive that Thou art a prophet"; and declared to the villagers with pardonable exaggeration, "He told me all that I have done," and asked, "Is not He the Christ?" The conclusion was perhaps a little precipitate but, as it turned out, the impulsive confession of faith from the lips of the peasant woman was correct, while the unbelief of the more hesitant and critical turned out to be tragic error.

To repeat yet once again, we do not see with the eyes but with the mind and all the equipment of the mind. Indeed the Samaritan woman saw not so much with eyes or mind but with her heart. "The heart," says Pascal, "has reasons of its own," and we may add "a power of vision of its own." Tennyson speaks of "heart and mind according well," and it may be true to say that the mind cannot see without the heart. At least one must love Truth before he can see Truth. Charles Bigg in his incomparable Introduction to the *Confessions of St. Augustine,* says the Saint reached his conclusion by "throwing his heart into the scales." "Thou shalt love the Lord thy God with thy whole mind and with thy whole heart," says the Savior. If we can love with the mind we can see with the heart. Those who stand aloof demanding that truth shall take them by assault, battering their minds into submission will in most cases be disappointed. Or should we rather say "not disappointed"? Perhaps it would disappoint and distress them if they were to be convinced.

There was a second group of hearers, friendly to a certain degree with Jesus, but who felt that they couldn't go all the way with Him. They enjoyed His parables. They admired His discourses. They marveled at His miracles. It did not scandalize them that He was poor or that the intellectual elite discounte-nanced Him.

But when He spoke in a vein too deeply spiritual or mystical for them they said "This is a hard saying and who can bear it?" Some of them, says St. John, "walked no more with Him." The Eucharist proved too much for them: "How can this man give us His flesh to eat?" Also there were apparent blasphemies: "Before Abraham was made, I am"; "The Father and I are one"; or His seeming intolerance, "No man cometh to the Father except by Me." As time went on He lost more and more of them until at the end He had the allegiance of very few.

Their counterpart is to be found today even among Church-going Christians. They are like the man who, being asked how far a gentleman should go in religion, answered "Not too far." They have an affectionate devotion to "the Nazarene," but they prefer that one should not put to them the penetrating question: "What think you of Christ? Whose Son is He?" If it happens that His terrifying declaration that one who divorces and marries again is in adultery applies to them, they reserve to themselves the right to interpret and to apply that devastating utterance.

As with Christ so with the Church that claims to be His. There are those who appreciate what she has done for the betterment of society and indeed for the civilization of the world, but who feel that she is only one among many philanthropic, humanitarian organizations. In particular they find it difficult to accept or even understand the phrase, "The Church, the Mystical Body of Christ." They have read St. Paul and they admire him, but some-how his teachings, so often reiterated as to be a key doctrine that the Church is Christ, baffles them. So would St. Augustine's epigram (enigmatic to the uninitiated), "The Church is Christ preaching Christ," or Bossuet's "The Church is Jesus Christ . . . whole and entire." This is obviously a mystical, or as St. Paul says a spiritual, concept; and as he says again "the carnal man [shall we say the common sense, matter-of-fact man] savoreth not the things that are of the spirit."

"Modern man," especially perhaps modern man in the Western world, is familiar with the ideas, "organization," "institution," "philanthropic," "educational," "humanitarian," but he balks at the expression "Mystical Body of Christ."

Cardinal Suhard of Paris, in a striking passage of a pastoral letter, amplifies the idea of St. Paul: "The visible Church is the Son of God Himself, everlastingly manifesting Himself among men in a human form, perpetually renovated and eternally young —the permanent incarnation of the Son of God." To the "modern man" this is unintelligible. In another passage the Cardinal continues: "Envisaged in its substantial reality the Church is definitive and perfect. She is all holy, fully perfect. As the immortal prolongation of the Savior in time, she conserves the essential of His resurrection: 'I am with you all days even to the consummation of the world.' The sacred desposit of Revelation which Tradition transmits from century to century remains absolutely intact and immutable in her. She is truly the New Law of which not an iota shall be changed, the Message whose words shall not pass. The Church is a rock and a norm which escapes changes. No attack injures her, no temptation corrupts her. Considered from this angle she adds nothing to Christ, she only makes Him visible in His infinite reality."

To many friendly non-Catholics that passage seems to be hopelessly idealistic, not to say untrue and absurd. So, in the end, those who look upon us from outside remain dissenters, courteous dissenters and reluctant, but none the less in the original sense of the word protestants. Their protest is not violent or malicious. Perhaps they would prefer not to call it a protest at all, but a confession of nescience, as in the case of those who, confronted with any mysticism whatsoever, say "it is beyond my depth."

However, Cardinal Suhard's description of the Church cannot fall upon the ears of Scripture readers as preposterous, unheard of, blasphemous. It is, after all, only an elaboration of the text in St. Paul: "A glorious Church, not having spot or wrinkle or any such thing but that it should be holy and without blemish." It was St. Paul, after all, not modern theologians or medieval mystics, who first expressed the idea of the Church as the Body of Christ, the risen Body that can no longer be slain or even wounded. The great apostle was anything but blind to the defects of the Christian people, but he held that their sins could not touch or tarnish the Mystical Body of Jesus Christ.

All of which, no doubt, is equivalent to saying that no one wholly deprived of the mystical temperament, and hence of supernatural faith, can *see* the Church—that is, comprehend it in its essence. To such a one it may not be inappropriate to say, as Turner did to the lady who exclaimed "I never saw any such sunset as *that*!"—"Don't you wish you could?"

Those who cannot "see" the Church, in the sense indicated, remain at a loss to explain her supernatural vigor after so many centuries of life and of conflict. That phenomenon has to be explained.

Chapter 15

The Church They Do Not See

IF I were to offer advice to one who feels impelled to write a book against the Catholic Church, I might repeat the famous advice of *Punch* "To Those About to be Married: Don't!" Or I might retell the anecdote, doubtless apocryphal, of a Cardinal in Rome who, meeting an anti-Catholic propagandist, said: "I understand that your aim is to destroy the Catholic Church. Don't try it. It's no use. Here in Rome we have been attempting to do just that for fifteen hundred years. We have not succeeded. Neither will you."

The enemies of the Church have less chance than her friends of dealing her a mortal blow. "What are these wounds in the midst of Thy hands? With these was I wounded in the house of them that loved Me." The Church can be hurt only by her friends. She thrives on the attacks of enemies. Nothing vitalizes and rejuvenates her so much as persecution. Countries in which powerful blows were dealt her four hundred years ago are the countries in which she thrives today. Any decline in her vitality has been in lands where she has had little opposition.

Voltaire was a shrewd and powerful antagonist. He combined vicious onslaught with cutting satire. But his battle-cry, *Écrasez l'infâme* ("Destory the infamous thing"), spoken of the Church, remains unrealized. There is today a Catholic revival in Voltaire's land. In fact there is always a Catholic revival. In England, to give another example, 400 years after the Elizabethan Inquisition, Catholics increase while the Established Church decreases. The poet Dryden speaks of the Catholic Church as "the milk-white Hind . . . so often doomed to death but fated not to die."

William Lyon Phelps in an Introduction to George Shuster's *The World's Great Catholic Literature,* quotes from the Pope's speech in "The Ring and the Book" the line, "I must survive a thing ere know it dead." It would be wiser of our antagonists if they would wait and explain what killed the Church than to set forth prematurely the reasons why she is not fit to live. When Leo XIII died, one of the many eulogists who declared that the dead pope left the Church vastly stronger than he found her, was Goldwin Smith. Whereupon Felix Adler of the Ethical Society group recalled that Goldwin Smith had said thirty-three years earlier when Pius IX lost its temporal power, "This marks the end of the papacy."

When I was a child of six or eight years, I used to sit sometimes in wonder before a steel engraving of the death of Pope Pius IX with the enigmatic—to me—inscription: "The Pope does not die." The pope was dying but the pope doesn't die! The enigma was soon resolved as the boy grew older. For anti-Catholic wishful thinkers it seems never to be resolved. "O pope I shall be the death of thee," said Martin Luther. Today in Berlin alone there are 700,000 Catholics and in all Germany half the population adheres to the pope.

Those who are bent on doing away with the Church would save themselves much unprofitable labor if they would read her history. Commencing away back, they would learn of Nero's edict, "You are not allowed to exist." Nero was a bungler and so was Caligula. But the last two persecutors, Decius and Diocletian, went at the business of blotting out Catholicism systematically. Where Nero slew his hundreds Diocletian slew huudreds of thousands. But after Diocletian came Constantine, and today at the Vatican *in perpetuam rei memoriam* you may see the busts of all the emperors who tried to kill the Church and portraits of their successors throughout the centuries.

The Church which can be harmed only by her own, can be understood only by her own. In that she is not unique. No people, country, nation can be justly judged by outsiders. Take our own country. What critic from Europe or Asia can speak accurately of America and Americans? Those who should know us best, the English, are perhaps the last to appreciate American institutions, customs, manners, the entire American ethos. "Whether you like it or not," said Hilaire Belloc to an audience of English and Americans in London, "we are getting further apart all the time." The nearer we seem the remoter we are. The unmannerly insults of old-fashioned Britishers like Charles Dickens and Mrs. Trollope, are no longer the vogue, but many of those who come to us from the "mother country" to enjoy our hospitality and our generosity, return home to ridicule and vituperate all things American. There is scarcely a book, newspaper, magazine, published in England which does not contain habitually or occasionally, descriptions of what dreadful people we Americans are and how abominably we conduct ourselves.

Especially when the critic from Albion prefaces his remarks with the phrase, "I like America, but—," his criticism will be unkind and unfair. Sitting at an Englishman's table in his own home (and hence inhibited by the code of good manners from denying or disputing) I had to listen to his castigation of an American who had said to my host after the first World War, "It is only fair that we Americans should give our money, since you English gave your blood." The Englishman said, "Imagine! Comparing your money with our blood!" A perverse twist to a well intended remark.

I would not say nor imply that all foreign observers err so outrageously, but it is probably true that no European can judge America accurately and justly. The rule works both ways. It is impossible for us to describe, still less to explain ourselves to Europeans, and they too probably feel frustrated when they try to explain themselves to us.

What applies to peoples applies *a fortiori* to Churches. So, it might be well for citizens of one nation to observe in regard to another nation and members of one Church in regard to another, what the wise little book, *The Imitation of Christ,* suggests in the relationship of man with man. "In judging others a man toileth in vain, for the most part he is mistaken and he easily sinneth; but judging and scrutinizing himself, he always laboreth with profit." To that rule St. Francis de Sales adds another: "Beware of judging those whom you do not like." To add a third: "Don't make invidious comments upon those whom you may possibly envy or of whom you may be jealous."

Together with facts, the motives of the hostile critic are important. Facts in themselves are largely neutral; they can be interpreted variously, and the interpretation may depend upon a motive hidden deep in the critic's unconscious mind. Two or three years ago there appeared a pretentious attack on the Catholic Church, professedly in regard solely to her alleged hostility to American freedom. The secular reviews almost unanimously praised especially the "careful documentation" of the work. But a Catholic defense (appearing unfortunately not until a year later) easily demonstrated that the author of the attack didn't understand his own documentation. Documents even more than facts need understanding. If the critic has a thesis in his head and a prejudice in his heart, he cannot rightly interpret his own sources. Two generations ago a learned Philadelphian, Henry C. Lea, wrote on the anti-Catholic side about "The Inquisition," "Celibacy," "Confession," "Indulgences." His work was scholarly, but a greater scholar (especially in those matters) the Abbé Hogan, replied briefly that if Dr. Lea had only stepped into a Catholic rectory, any priest would have explained to him how he had misunderstood much of his admittedly imposing documentation. The truth is that the non-Catholic, who (perhaps unknown to himself) is by tradition and, so to speak, by blood, anti-

Catholic, cannot see the Church. He looks at the Church, scruti-nizes, analyzes, judges and condemns—but he doesn't *see*.

Romano Guardini, in his excellent study of Christ, *The Lord,* says: "Seeing is a vital process; to see means to submit to the in-fluence of things, to place oneself within their grasp. Necessarily the will mounts guard over the vision. On the whole we see what we choose to see. This being true on the natural plane, how much truer it is on the spiritual. To see another human being as he really is means to lay ourselves open to his influence. When fear or dislike moves us to avoid him, this reaction is already evident in our gaze: the eye caricaturizes him, stifling the good, height-ening the bad. We discern his intentions, make swift comparisons and leap to conclusions. The deeper our fear or distrust of a person the more tightly we close our eyes to him until finally we are incapable of perception or the profound German word for it *Wahrnehmen,* reception-of-truth. We have become blind to that particular person. This mysterious process lies behind every enmity. Discussion, preaching, explanations are utterly useless. The eye simply ceases to register what is plain to be seen. The mind must turn to justice, the heart expand, then only can the eye see to discern."

"The eye must turn to justice," says Guardini. He might have gone on to say not only to justice but to love. There we come face to face with a fundamental Gospel truth. Unless we love we cannot see. Perhaps no one can see, in the sense of discern, take into oneself, grasp, understand the Church unless he loves the Church. A hostile outsider cannot so much as see the Church.

Chapter 16

The Church and the Criminal

A YOUNG criminal, turning desperado after having murdered one policeman and mortally wounding another, skulked among the backyards, fences and dumps of a Chicago slum. The police, closing in on him, persuaded his sister to broadcast a message: "Johnny, this is your sister; I beg of you to go into the Church, surrender yourself to the priest, make your confession and take your chances with the law." That message was not only blared from the loud speaker of the patrol car, but was carried over television, with pictures of the girl, the police and the backyards, to millions of people. Reactions in the mind of hearers were varied. I remember one which expresses a point of view that many good people hold, but that seems to me un-Christian. "What a shame," said a pious woman, "that the Church, the priest, the Sacrament of Penance should be publicized in connection with a murder."

I do not feel that way. Rather it seems to me that the good lady was echoing the pharisaical complaint, "This man eateth and drinketh with sinners." The Church does not abhor criminals. She is the Church of "the poor," and to her, sinners are the poor; criminals and murderers are the poor. Like her Master she ministers to lepers, physical and moral, paying no attention to the cry "Unclean! unclean!" No one is less given to sentimentality than the Church; no one more firmly impressed by the truth of personal responsibility for sin and crime. Yet it is the Church that originated the phrase "intolerance for sin but tolerance for the sinner."

The Church refuses to excommunicate or anathematize criminals. She is aware that such tolerance damages her reputation among the pharisaical, as the reputation of her Master was damaged in the mind of Simon who said, "If this man were a prophet He would know what manner of woman" is this Magdalen. Finding fault with the Church because she retains the wicked in her fold seems to me substantially identical with the sin of the fastidious who disowned Christ because a mob of derelicts followed Him. Such snobbishness in the moral and spiritual plane seems even more un-Christian than in the social and financial world. It is strange that pious people can read the Gospels and not discover what Jesus was about, and the method He followed to achieve His purpose. He said plainly enough, "I am come to save not the just but sinners." Was He to save them by banishing them from His presence?

Our Lord rubbed elbows with sinners, felt the pressure and caught the aroma of their unwashed bodies as they crowded close to Him. He was under no illusion as to their moral condition. "He knew what was in man." He was aware that they were not nice people. But He preferred contact with them rather than with the social and intellectual elite. He could have formed an academy of philosophers after the fashion of Socrates. He could have claimed a rostrum in the precincts of the Temple: it was His Father's house. But He preferred the streets, the open road, the hillside. As for personal contact with sinners, that was his delight. He could not abide those who "trusted in themselves and despised others."

St. Paul, some years later was to confess that the Christians of his congregation were *peripsema*—offscourings. Anyone who imagines that Jesus and Paul should have devoted themselves to congregations of aristocrats, and that either the Savior or the Apostle shared the sentiment of Horace, *odi profanum vulgus et arceo* (I hate the common horde and I avoid them), has missed the Message entirely.

Some one has said—indeed a great many close students of the Gospels and Epistles have said—that the Gospel is an incentive to social revolution. One modern sociologist stated, "Christianity is a social revolution and it is nothing else." These professors, ostensibly devoted to exact thinking and cautious expression, do make such wild statements! But we must confess that the sociologists' dictum has in it a glimmer of truth. St. James in his Catholic Epistle says: "If there shall come into your assembly a man having a golden ring, in fine apparel, and there shall come in also a poor man in mean attire, and you have respect to him that is clothed with the fine apparel and shall say to him: Sit thou here well, but say to the poor man stand out there or sit under my footstool . . . are ye not become unjust judges. Hath not God chosen the poor in this world rich in faith and heirs to the kingdom? But you have dishonored the poor man." In another chapter James, who by the way was the Lord's cousin, pours it on: "Go to now, ye rich men and howl in your miseries. Your riches are corrupted and your garments are moth-eaten; your gold and silver is cankered . . . you have stirred up to yourselves wrath against the last days." It would be interesting to know how often sermons on that text are preached in that mood to congregations of "nice people," and how much adroit exegesis is employed to make the message inoffensive to pious ears.

However we were on the subject not of poor people but of sinners and criminals in the Church. As Lazarus the beggar was the type of poor man who found rest in Abraham's bosom, Mary Magdalen represents all sinners who came close to Jesus and were not driven away, and the "good thief," a robber and murderer, represents all criminals whom Christ and His Church refuse to reprobate. Here and there in the early Church there were puritanical groups who held that certain sins—adultery, idolatry, apostasy—were unforgivable. The Church promptly rejected such rigorism and to the scandal of the *unco guid* she has ever since declined to refuse anyone, no matter how wicked, access to her. She is not unaware that for such leniency she incurs opprobrium. But she remembers that Christ endured and survived disdain, and so will she. To those who are fond of anathemas and excommunications she says, "You know not of what spirit you are." There are those who think the Church intolerant, and if tolerance is understood to be acceptance of error in the realm of doctrine, she is intolerant. But she is the least intolerant of all religious bodies in providing a refuge for moral outcasts. She appropriates the words of Her Founder, "Come to me all you that labor and are weary [come unto me all you that are sinful] and you shall find rest for your souls."

In the hymn "The New Jerusalem" it is said, "All who would might enter and no one was denied." That generous sentiment seems to contradict the Lord's words about "sheep" and "goats," or "come ye blessed, depart ye cursed." But into the Kingdom of God on earth all may enter and no one is denied.

It would be interesting and perhaps profitable to seek an answer to the question: how many of those who become superficially acquainted with the Church remain alienated because of her predilection for the poor, the sinners, the uncouth, the vulgar, the uneducated, and, above all, her tolerance for the criminal? I have read and heard criticisms of the Church because of the number of her adherents who are in jails, reformatories, houses of correction. The argument would seem to be that if we cannot make all Catholics law-abiding we cannot be the Church of Christ. Such reasoning seems to be identical with that of the Pharisees. They were scandalized at the sight of the rag-tag and bob-tail who traipsed across the country on the heels of the Master. If He were what He claimed to be, why didn't He make saints of them all on the spot and in one instant? Since He could lay His hand upon a leper and cleanse him of his foul disease, why didn't He purify and sanctify all sinners with one glance?

Also, what about that embarrassing episode of the "good thief," who was also a murderer? Strange company for the Savior as He went out of this world into the next. Were the inhabitants of heaven also scandalized?

And how about all the other wicked people with whom our Savior came into contact? For one example, take the woman at the well in Samaria. "You have had five husbands," said Jesus, "and he whom you now have is not your husband." But the Lord didn't gather His garments about Him and say, "See that you touch Me not." It was the woman, adulteress and half heathen who was surprised: "How is it that you, a Jew, talk to me a Samaritan." And, she might have added, "not a good Samaritan at that." But He took the whole episode in stride, so to speak. There was no danger of contamination in her presence.

The Church seems to feel the same way. Sinners and criminals cannot drag her down. She may possibly lift them up. Other Christian organizations seem to be not so sure of themselves. They have to be careful of their reputation. They are afraid that "nice people" may think ill of them and turn away from them, if they tolerate the company of the wicked.

There was one woman whom I had instructed carefully and at considerable length, who admitted that she was convinced, but she said: "In your church one cannot worship without contact with all sorts of persons; elsewhere I meet such lovely people." So she joined the church of the lovely people.

Catholics have a curious feeling about that matter. If ever we become so aristocratic and so respectable that the poor and the sinners and the criminals keep away from us, we shall know that we have apostatized from the true faith.

I have mentioned in the beginning of this chapter the young criminal whose sister advertised to all the world that the boy was a Catholic. Shortly after that "scandalous" and "embarrassing" episode, there appeared in the daily press two other items of much the same purport. In one case a woman accused of conspiracy to murder was reported in the newspapers to have attended Mass on the day of the crime and to have spoken of praying to "The Blessed Mother." The other instance was that of a woman who had kidnapped a baby, but driven by conscience or by fear, gave the child into the keeping of a Catholic pastor. We could make an explanation if not a disclaimer of responsibility in such cases. But we don't. We accept the opprobrium deserved or undeserved. We remember the Mary Magdalen episode, that of the woman at the well, and the thief on the cross. So we avoid self-justification, and we feel we can say, as St. Paul did in another kind of matter, that we think we have the mind of Christ.

Chapter 17

The Church and "Progress"

VOLTAIRE wrote in one of his innumerable letters, "If there were no God, it would be necessary to invent Him." Not too many years after the appearance of that shrewd observation, as if in confirmation of it, the revolutionists in Paris, having dethroned God, declared a substitute—"Reason." But reason is an abstract philosophical sort of deity, so they personified it in a flesh and blood woman—a foul sort of woman by the way—and actually committed the sacrilege of placing her upon the altar at Notre Dame.

"Reason" as a god lasted but a short while. In our day Reason is fallen so low that no modern philosophical system gives her recognition, not to say a genuflection, still less an adoring prostration. Pragmatism, Vitalism, Freudianism, Behaviorism, all the new philosophies scout reason. They say we are not governed by reason but by impulse and indeed that all our thoughts and words and deeds, our "reactions," our sins and crimes and virtues, are all mechanically determined.

After Reason in place of God came Science, called more impressively "Modern Science." But science as a god is slipping. As long ago as 1890 Ferdinand Brunetière, a very notable thinker, declared science "bankrupt." A contemporary critic, Joseph Wood Krutch, who would be flattered if I called him the American Brunetière, after speaking of "the despair which has beset intelligent people in recent years," devotes a whole chapter in *The Modern Temper* to "Disillusion with the Laboratory." Back in the early years of the century Professor Loeb was promising to create life in the laboratory. But instead of life, death comes from the laboratory—hideous horrible death; and only the scientists who work in secret know what still more horrible kinds of death will come out of the laboratory to be utilized in the next war. Those who used to bend the knee to modern science have become so fearful of modern science that some of them have tried to call a halt—a moratorium they call it—on science. They want science to stop in its tracks and wait for ethics and morals to catch up. With science there was a twin-god, the Machine. Machinery was to revolutionize civilization. But the machine, now become incredibly high powered, threatens to get out of hand and smash man who made it. Another substitute for God, contemporary with the machine and with science, was Evolution. "Some call it Evolution, others call it God," says Carruthers, and irrational though it be, there still are persons who think that Evolution can perform all the functions of God, and that since we have evolution we may dispense with the hypothesis of any other deity.

Herbert Spencer was the high priest of the religion of Evolution. High priest, prophet, philosopher, pedagogue, and factotum. He explained: "Human society which starts from the condition in which each family wanders about alone and isolated, and each man at once warrior, hunter, fisherman, tool-maker and builder, shall pass through the nomadic stage in which several families are united in a kind of chieftainship where the king is at once judge and king, and eventuate in those complex settled states of Modern Civilization where labour is carried to its minutest subdivision and every function finds its appropriate social organ."

But Thomas Huxley, who was an even better expositor of Darwinism than Herbert Spencer, admitted, or rather emphasized, the fact that the evolutionary process is non-moral. Evolutionary progress, he declared, wars against social progress, ethical progress, moral progress, and hence the progress of civilization.

So if evolution is a god it is a non-moral god, a heedless, heartless, remorseless god. Tennyson saw that, he says:

> . . . Nature red in tooth and claw
> With rapine, shrieked against his creed

the creed of man who thought that God was love. Shall man

> Who loved, who suffered countless ills,
> Who battled for the True, the Just,
> Be blown about the desert dust
> Or sealed within the iron hills?

If that be the end of evolution, man, says Tennyson (and I dare say, also God), would be

> . . . A monster then, a dream,
> A discord. Dragons of the prime,
> That tear each other in their slime,
> Were mellow music matched with him.

But the saddest, most tragic, most hopeless conclusion, if there be no God but Evolution, is that of Bertrand Russell who speaks of "Omnipotent matter, blind to good and evil, reckless of destruction, rolling on its relentless way"; and who has epitomized the pessimism inherent in the evolution-theory in a passage as eloquent as it is despondent:

"Man is the product of causes which had no prevision of the end they were achieving; his origin, his growth, his hopes and fears, his loves and his beliefs, are but the outcome of accidental collocations of atoms; no fire, no heroism, no intensity of thought and feeling, can preserve an individual life beyond the grave; all the labors of the ages, all the devotion, all the inspiration, all the noon-day brightness of human genius, are destined to extinction in the vast death of the solar system; and the whole temple of Man's achievement must inevitably be buried beneath the debris of a universe in ruins."

As a kind of fillip to that horrifying prophecy of the ultimate
fate of man, H. G. Wells, once the favorite spokesman of semi-
educated worshippers at the shrine of Evolution, says that he
looks upon the world as "a very dire and terrible world" and that
hope has been all but extinguished from his heart.

"Reason" and "Science" and "The Machine" and "Evolution"
having all disappointed the human race, there remains an un-
daunted though unsubstantiated belief in "Progress." Those who
worship Progress make an act of faith in the proposition that the
universe and man move ever onward and upward from chaos to
order, from the amoeba, a splotch of protoplasmic jelly in a pud-
dle of mud, to that highly complex and intricate organism, man.
Herbert Spencer gave a classic definition of evolutionary progress
in a paragraphic sentence which we all had to memorize when
we were in college. I will not repeat it here—it is too long and
too difficult to follow—but the gist of it is that all things that
exist pass from the simple to the multiform, from the incoherent
to the coherent, from the indefinite to the definite, and so on.
What it really means is that the universe with all its worlds and
all its solar systems, with all vegetable, animal, and human life,
is constantly, everlastingly ascending, moving steadily forward
to a goal of unlimited perfection.

The trouble is, of course, that not only individuals but entire
races of men and indeed whole civilizations go downward and
backward as well as upward and onward. The archaeologist will
tell you that the surface of the earth is heavily encumbered with
ruins. If you dig down some 15 or 20 feet below the surface of
the sands in Egypt or in Babylonia, you will find buried remnants
of what used to be magnificent, gorgeous civilizations. In Athens
the ruins stare at you gaunt and pathetic from the top of the hill
of Mars like broken tombstones: in the Forum at Rome you see
them again, beautiful in a kind of way, but none the less tragic
reminders that a civilization like a man dies and rots in the earth.
Indeed they say that beneath the surface of the city of Rome

there are deeper and deeper layers, nine in all, one dead civilization laid upon the ruins of another, as the bones of a man may be
laid in a grave above those of his father, and the father's in turn
upon those of his father. Edward Gibbon tells, in the familiar
preface to his masterpiece *The Decline and Fall of the Roman
Empire,* of his sad musings at the ruins of the Coliseum. He
didn't put his thoughts into verse but Kipling has done it for
him:

> The tumult and the shouting dies,
> The captains and the kings depart . . .
> All valiant dust that builds on dust.

The prophet Isaias wrote it a thousand years before Rome was
ruined. "All flesh is grass and all the glory thereof as the flower
of the field. The grass is withered and the flower is fallen . . .
indeed the people is grass"; and, to complete the thought from
our Savior Himself, the "Grass that is today and tomorrow is
cast into the oven." For those who do not read Isaias or the
Gospels, there is, again, H. G. Wells, who wrote shortly after
World War I:

"The system under which we have grown up, the system we
call modern civilization, is heading very rapidly downhill towards
disaster, and people living as we do are not realizing with any
strength of conviction just what that downward movement
amounts to. I have seen a modern civilized system broken down.
I saw railways falling out of use. I saw a great city visibly dying,
houses tumbling down, roads falling into the drains below, all
the methods of urban transport going out of use. That process
of collapse has spread."

In a book which in its day made a vast impression, *The Decline
of the West,* Oswald Spengler denies that civilization as a whole,
world-wide civilization, develops constantly. In fact he denies that
there is any one universal civilization. There are many successive
civilizations which spring up here and there, develop, decline,

die like individual men, and (if I read him rightly) he seems to say that after all we don't really get anywhere. For whole civilizations, as for individual men, "The path of glory leads but to the grave." When some evolutionists in Darwin's day said that although individuals are blotted out, the "type" goes on, Tennyson answered, speaking of Nature,

> So careful of the type, but no.
> From scarped cliff and quarried stone
> She cries, "A thousand types are gone:
> I care for nothing, all shall go."

To consider a phenomenon closer at hand and more easily verifiable, do we not see before our very eyes certain signs of the criminality of our own American people? We commit more murders than all Europe combined, and our homicide rate is five times that of England. We grind out more divorces than any country in Europe. The institution of the family, the basis of civilized society and of the State, is riddled, say rather in some classes of society, destroyed. We lead the world with embezzlers, grafters, gangsters, racketeers, hijackers, kidnappers. To our terrible disgrace there have been nearly 5000 lynchings in the United States north and south, since 1882. In spite of the expenditure of uncountable millions of dollars on popular education, the mass of the people remain easy victims of almost any demagogue, provided he be sufficiently dogmatic, blatant, violent, intolerant, or on the other hand charming, fascinatingly hypnotic in personality and in speech. It is notorious that the people at large are governed here and now by emotion, passion, and not by reason, notwithstanding a hundred years of common school, high school and college education.

As for sex-sins, natural and unnatural, normal and abnormal, you will have to ask the custodians of clinics and of insane asylums for the horrible statistics and the ghastly details. Together with all this, we have our share (more than a proper share for a young nation) of social and economic ills—five major depressions or panics in one man's lifetime, and that in a land bursting with natural resources.

I present these unpleasant facts not to make an indictment against my own nation, but in the interest of truth and to give pause to those evolutionistic moderns who cry "Progress!"—as if Progress were as plain as a mountain rising in magnificent solitude from a plain, and as undeniable as the sun in a cloudless sky at noonday.

I believe in Progress myself and my Church believes in Progress. But belief in Progress demands an act of faith. It isn't as plain as A. B. C., or as evident as twice 2 make 4. I believe in Progress because and only because I believe in God. Blot out God and I couldn't believe in Progress because there would be neither a starting point from which progress could begin nor a goal towards which progress could aim. And worse still, if there were no God there could be no guiding hand to direct the way of man and the Universe. The world and all on it would be in the same danger as the sun when the inexperienced Phaeton drove it madly across the skies.

In a word, the Church refuses to share the tragic and pitiable despondency of the Oswald Spenglers, the Bertrand Russells, the Herbert George Wellses, and of the astronomers who think the world is running down, because the Church believes in God, the only God not Science as God, not Evolution as God, not Progress as God, but the one only God, the God Who creates and inspires true science, directs the true evolution, and controls the progress of the spheres through space and of man to his eternal goal.

PART V

CHRISTIANITY THE TOUCHSTONE

Essays in Practical Ethics

Chapter 18

The Individual and the Organization

EVER since the beginning of the mechanical age, the idea has been current that eventually man would be dominated and destroyed by a machine of his own making. The notion has given rise to at least one literary masterpiece, Mary Shelley's weird romance, *Frankenstein*. There is also a suggestion of the same theme in Eugene O'Neill's morbid drama, *Dynamo*. Frankenstein, it will be remembered, succeeded in creating a soulless monster, a fiend that pursued its maker implacably to his end. And in Eugene O'Neill's play, the chief character (one can hardly call him hero), having cast aside God, prays to the Dynamo, worships it and finally immolates himself to the mechanical deity by thrusting his hands into the live wires.

The idea is as fascinating as it is gruesome. And the time has come, I think, for some novelist or dramatist to tell of the conflict of man with the most relentless machine of all—the political, industrial, financial, social machine which I ask permission to call broadly "Organization."

I hope I need not waste words in explaining that I am not opposed to organization as such. Only an anarchist, a nihilist or the most extravagant individualist could think to dispense with organization. Even savages have an embryonic organization, the tribe. And as civilization becomes complex, the need of organization becomes greater. In fact all society, industrial, mercantile, political, is a vast network of organization.

However, there is a danger of our being hyperorganized. The

machine made by man's hands may destroy man's soul. In a world pyramided with organization upon organization, a man needs the strength of Atlas to prevent the crushing out of his personality and individuality. Indeed, to drop the metaphor of the pyramid and resume that of the machine, if a person is to remain a person and not occupy the place of a cog or a nut or a bolt or a gadget of some kind, he must constantly remind himself that he is flesh and blood, body and soul and conscience, and not a piece of inanimate metal that clicks back and forth when some one turns a switch or pushes a lever.

Take for example, a man—an honorable man—who goes into politics. Let us say he has talent, force, independence, character. He is master of his own soul and keeper of his own conscience. He is, without affectation, a patriot. He could say—but he doesn't because he hates even the suspicion of cant—that he enters his country's service for his country's good. Being something of an idealist he feels a sense of consecration when he takes his first oath of office, almost like that of a priest vowing himself to a sacred cause. Long ago Paul Leicester Ford wrote a novel, *The Honorable Peter Stirling,* with such a hero. Peter passes unscathed and untarnished through the lesser municipal offices and becomes a "boss" with clean hands and a clean conscience. Today the mention of a clean-handed, clean-hearted political "boss" sounds incredible, perhaps ridiculous. We have seen too many bright young fellows of good mental and moral character, plunging into politics and coming out covered with muck and mire, or, more likely, not coming out at all but remaining and floundering around in the morass of corruption.

I remember years ago saying to a friend of mine when a man of particularly high principle was elected to a great office: "That's the type. Thank heaven, we now have a man worthy of the job." The answer was disquieting: "Don't be so sure. I know him better than you do. They will wear him down. They will wear him down!"

Too often the cynical prophecy is verified. The clean-cut conscience becomes blunted; the fine principles are abandoned one by one as Quixotic; the ethical ideals which our hero and patriot used to proclaim without blushing and with no reason to blush, come to seem childish even to himself, like the priggish maxims of an old-fashioned copy book. In their place he has an entirely new philosophy, new on his lips but in itself as old as politics. His new code runs something like this: "It's a hard game. When you're in the game you must play the game as the game is played. In politics there is always a *quid pro quo,* something for something, nothing for nothing, give and take. You give a favor and you take your compensation—not necessarily monetary compensation. 'Graft'? What do you mean? Emoluments? Honorariums? Little friendly recognitions from constituents for favors received? An occasional voluntary offering, let us say a checking account or a stock account (without responsibility) as a present from a friend who wonders how you can meet your obligations on an inadequate salary? Friend, call it not 'Graft,' that is a rude word; call it 'perquisites pertaining to the office.' It is the custom, and do not even professors of ethics in your most reputable universities teach that customs make morals and that morality consists of conformity with custom?"

However, to one principle even the most hardened politician remains true: "Be loyal!" But loyal to what? To conscience? To high principle? To the ideals with which you began? Don't be foolish. Be loyal to the organization! What you hear and see and know within the organization that wouldn't sound nice in public, keep to yourself. If you feel like making accusations, make them against the other party, never against your own. When a campaign is on you may have to speak in behalf of a man you know to be a rascal, but suppress the ugly truth, sound his praises; tell the people that the honorable gentleman whose name you are about to mention has by his services and his character merited the support of every forward-looking citizen. Say it if it chokes you. In a word, be regular. Never, never, as you value your political career, never bolt the party. It may be rotten to the core. You may know in your heart that a change of administration would be good. But admit nothing. Say—and say it without the flicker of a smile—that all the patriots are of your party and all the incompetents in the other.

So in conformity with this demoralizing code, our high-minded young fellow loses, somewhere between his entrance into politics and the achievement of his goal, all the idealism he ever possessed. He stupefies his conscience, stultifies his reason. He falls to the level of the law of the jungle: "For the law of the jungle is this; that the wolf must hunt with the pack."

In a word he is just one more victim of the organization. The organization has swallowed the individual, body, bones, hide, hair. His identity as an independent, intelligent, responsible human being is lost.

As with politics, so in a lesser degree (though I know some who would say in a *greater* degree) with business. John T. Flynn opens his book *Graft in Business* with this pistol shot: "The average politician is a rank amateur in the gentle art of graft, compared with his brother in the field of business." He admits that such a declaration seems like "preposterous exaggeration," but he goes on to quote the Federal Trade Commission and other reliable sources in proof of his statement. The journal, *Commerce and Finance* says, for example:

"Federal investigations have shown the prevalence of commercial bribery which has been allowed to flourish unchecked because of a lack of adequate laws to put a stop to it. The secret giving of commissions or other things to employees of customers to induce them to buy or recommend the purchase of certain supplies has become a nation-wide system. It infests not only the ordinary lines of business but also the professions, even the surgical profession . . . Waiving the moral issues involved—a fact few will dispute—a practice authoritatively estimated to take a billion dollars a year out of the cash drawer of business should be stamped out for strictly business reasons."

And he adds: "The general manager of the New York Better Business Bureau confirms this estimate of a billion-dollar-a-year cost to business, and to business in New York City alone at least a hundred million."

Now, face to face with such facts as these, the individual realizes that business can be a machine which grinds down his honor, his independence and his conscience. A young man, fresh from a fine home, college, school, where he has learned a noble ethic, finds himself confronted by principles and practices which seem to him dishonest or dubious, but which he gradually comes to accept as inevitable. The business world, like the political world, "wears him down, wears him down."

As an employee he finds advancement delayed if he shows himself squeamish or scrupulous about the methods that prevail in his organization. Young men in business, like young men in politics, are supposed not to be hoity-toity, and not to assume a holier-than-thou attitude. "Business is business" is the slogan in many a house, and the slogan covers a multitude of methods that would shock a pristine-pure conscience. He is taken aside and given what purports to be friendly advice: "See here, young fellow, buckle down to work and forget the maxims you read in Poor Richard's Almanac. Ben Franklin is dead. Not only dead but debunked, like a lot of other pharisaical business men who, having made their pile, turned in their old age to writing hypocritical mottoes for schoolboys." And before long his conscience is bent, if not broken.

I hope I do not seem unsympathetic with the fine young fellows who go forth into the world of affairs and find themselves face to face with organized dishonesty. I realize full well how hard it is to "hew to the line" in business and in politics under contemporary conditions. Nor is the Church unsympathetic. She is an old Church, a wise and kindly Church. She does not lack understanding. But she is relentless in her insistence that the individual conscience must not be sacrificed to custom. With that in mind she offers expert and disinterested advice in matters of business and political ethics to all who make use of the confessional. In Catholic moral theology the Treatise on Justice and Right is held to be perhaps the most important and incidentally the most difficult of all. Furthermore the popes have in recent years again and again laid down the principles of social justice which Catholics are supposed to observe.

Finally, the Church appeals to the religious motive: She preaches that the ready-made maxims of the worldly-wise who attempt to justify what is essentially dishonest will not avail before God, and that if one were to attempt to speak them in the Judgment his tongue would cleave to the roof of his mouth. And as all the Catholic people can testify, there is no text more familiar in our Church than this: "What doth it profit a man if he gain the whole world but suffer the loss of his own soul?"

Chapter 19

Patriotism Good and Bad

I USED to know a man who held that the greatest menace to civilization was patriotism. He was a good man and intelligent. He dearly loved to argue and he was profoundly sincere. He read a good deal, especially along the line of economics. In that subject he leaned towards radicalism. But he was orthodox in religion. His morality was beyond question. He was a good father to his family and until sickness came upon him in his latter years he was successful in business. He was, I should say, what Theodore Roosevelt used to call a "Desirable Citizen." So his indictment of patriotism was startling.

But, what the good man meant by "patriotism" was not a well-reasoned love of one's own country, its customs, its institutions, and its people, but a combative, truculent patriotism, which, pharisaically, trusts in itself and despises others; an illiberal, intolerant patriotism, the patriotism of the provincial who goes abroad and comes home filled with contempt of foreigners; the patriotism of the traveler with a closed mind who, after one visit to another continent, forever after makes invidious contrasts between older civilizations and our own, always to the advantage of our own; the patriotism of the ignoramus who visits a European art gallery, declares in a loud voice that the masterpieces are ridiculous, and who in a hotel lobby or at a sidewalk cafe tells the world that we do this or that better at home; or of the young fellow who saw in Rome, as he said, "nothing but ruins," and who considered the Yankee Stadium a greater marvel than the Coliseum; or of the vulgarian American who calls all other peoples by offensive nick-names; or of the old-fashioned Fourth of July orator who, red in the face and dripping perspiration, gesticulates and vociferates that we are the greatest people on earth and that we can lick all the rest of the world taken together; the patriotism in a word of that obnoxious type of Super-American who refers to our land as "God's Own Country" and to all other places as the land that God forgot.

That, I think, is what my late lamented friend had in mind when he denounced "patriotism" as the greatest menace to peace and to the progress of mankind; and I think we can all agree with him. When Doctor Johnson made his famous definition of patriotism as "the last refuge of a scoundrel," he might have added "or if not a scoundrel—a fool," and it may be debated whether fools or scoundrels do more harm.

Patriotism in its purity is, after religion, perhaps the highest and noblest of virtues. But in accordance with the Latin axiom, *"corruptio optimi pessima"* (which we may perhaps venture to translate in the current idiom, "the higher they stand the harder they fall"—the harder and the lower), there is scarcely anything more deplorable than a perverted or corrupted patriotism. A true patriot sings of the land that God gave to his fathers, "I love thy rocks and rills, thy woods and templed hills." And he adds what the poet omitted: "I love the people who climb thy hills and worship in thy temples. I love the earth on which I tread and I love the people who tread that same earth with me; I love not only the hills and rocks but the farms and the fields, the city streets, and the men who till the soil of those farms and fields and who walk those streets; I love those with whom I touch elbows in the streets and in public conveyances. At work and at play, in times of sorrow and of joy, in days of national humiliation when my country has suffered some calamity, and in days of jubilation consequent upon some triumph of war or of peace, I feel these men to be my brethren, like those who are my brothers according to the flesh, children from the womb of my mother. My heart is too big to be content with love of myself; it pours out its affection upon my family, my neighbors, acquaintances, fellow workers, fellow sufferers; upon all those whose eyes behold the same landscape as I, the same rivers and lakes and seas and mountains; who draw their sustenance, with me, from that same earth and those same waters. The soul within me is not dead. I do say 'This is my own, my native land'; indeed my 'heart within me burns' when I return from wandering on some foreign strand. If I have for a time been, though still within the borders of this vast country, far away from father, mother, brother, sister, my heart leaps and there is a catch in my throat as I approach my home once again; but an emotion no less spontaneous and scarcely less warm comes over me when I return from travel on some other continent than my own; and I feel an electric thrill pass through my frame when my foot touches once again my native soil."

All this is natural, and what is natural is God-given. Next to my religion, indeed part of my religion, is my patriotism. It is a sentiment, a passion, part of my being; it comes to me as an endowment from God Who made me. Quite as much as life, liberty and happiness, love of country is a divine gift and for that reason inalienable.

But the more noble and beautiful the sentiment, the more degraded and ignoble and ugly it becomes when perverted. Love, for example—love of man for woman and woman for man—is so sacred that Christ and the Church hold it a Sacrament. But when it is debased it becomes so loathsome that it is not to be mentioned among us. As with love of man for woman, so with love of man for God. There have been those in history and religion who, by some queer twist of mind, have thought that love of God involves hatred of man. They have hated and persecuted their fellows; have spoken all manner of evil against them; have driven them out of the synagogue and of other houses of worship; and doing so, have thought they did a service to God. This is the wildest, craziest, most cruel of all hatreds, hatred in the name of God and religion.

As with the love we have for another, as with the love we owe to God, so with the love we bear our country. It is in its pristine purity a beautiful and admirable sentiment. But if a patriot thinks himself called upon because he loves his country to hate some one else's country, he is no patriot. His kind of patriotism is indeed a menace.

Wars do not arise, as the disciples of Karl Marx or any other philosophic fatalist tell us, from economic causes: we are not caught in "the fell clutch of circumstance"; we are neither dumb-driven cattle nor are we machines set in motion when some one at a distance throws a switch to turn on an irresistible current. A man in a power house may take hold of a handle, thrust it up or pull it down and with that motion set ten thousand machines in motion or stop them. But no man, and by the same token no imaginary god of the heathens, Zeus or Moloch or Mars or Wotan, can look down over the ramparts of heaven, like a puppeteer looking down from the flies above the stage, pull a string and make us mortals dance and play or thrust and stab and kill as puppets do.

There comes to mind that tremendous word of Jesus, "It hath been said of old, thou shalt love thy neighbor and hate thy enemy, but I say to you, love your enemies." Tremendous doctrine! Revolutionary doctrine! "Impossible doctrine," says the cynic. But unless that sentence from the Sermon on the Mount is seen to be the basis of a genuine new order, this poor harassed old world will never have lasting peace. The "New Order" of Hitler or of Lenin-Trotsky-Stalin is not new; it is as old as warfare, it is warfare. Christ's New Order was new when He spoke it and it is new to this day, brand new; the nations have never used it. People are always asking, "What's wrong with the world?" The answer is so simple that when we give it the diplomats say "Too simple." They love to complicate matters; it is to their interest to keep things complicated. If international relationships ceased to be complicated, the diplomats would be out of a job. So they cry, *"Trop simpliste,"* "too simple," "too naive," "too unsophisticated," "too unrealistic," when we tell them that what's wrong with the world is that the world disagrees with God. But so long as they live by the outmoded maxim, "Love your friend, hate your enemy," they shall never have peace.

If the doctrine of the Sermon on the Mount is too highly mystical for us, if we give it lip service but inwardly disbelieve it, we can at least remember that less idealistic maxim of the apostle St. James, "The anger of man worketh not the justice of God"; and St. Paul's point-blank declaration that "The weapons of our warfare are not carnal." If the enemy lays waste the kingdom of God on earth we can build it up again. The Church has done so a dozen times before. But if we go into battle with the Cross in one hand and the sword in the other, the peoples whom we conquer will deride us as hypocrites when the battle is over; their resentments will survive the defeat of their arms, and the same unending series of war and revolutions will commence all over again. It is therefore the spirit of the Gospel and of the Church to favor a true sincere internationalism. But be it well understood —what the poet calls "the parliament of man, the federation of the world," cannot be established or maintained by physical force. The medieval league of nations, which we call "United Christendom," was possible—though to tell the truth the passions of men and the ambitions of kings hampered its activity—it was possible and feasible because Christendom recognized one head of the kingdom of God upon earth. But if you have for guarantee and sanction the rulings of the U.N., only a civil court implemented with arms, it will never succeed.

A League of Nations or a United Nations cannot build itself up and maintain its authority with what unthinking people call glibly an International Police Force. Such a police force is an army. You cannot hold Europe, Asia, Africa, America together with an army, any more than you can hold half a continent or a whole continent together with a Gestapo or a Cheka. But if you can persuade the people of one nation to love their own land and their own people first, and then expand that love until it embraces other nations and finally all nations, you will solve this problem of patriotism and superpatriotism, of nationalism and internationalism. But make no mistake about your method. You shall not bring that blessed Utopia to pass with arms. It will not spring up out of the earth when you have smashed a dictator or three dictators or a dozen. St. Gregory the Great in one of his homilies says in the laconic way of the early Romans, *"Contraria contrariis curantur"*—contraries are cured by contraries, intemperance by temperance, hatred by love, anger by patience, lust by continence. Force will be cured by gentleness, national and international antipathies will be overcome by love. It sounds unreal and impracticable. But it is the Gospel; the Gospel is Christ; and Christ the Son of God makes no mistake. We shall save the world His way or we shall not save it at all.

Chapter 20

Total Reform or None

THE world today is bewildered, not to say bedevilled, with a multiplicity of problems—political, social, economic, class, racial, local, national, international problems. Some say that because of modern inventions, which bring the ends of the earth closer together, all problems are world-wide. They tell us with some plausibility that we cannot solve the problems of the farmer who grows corn in Iowa unless at the same time we solve the problem, or at least grapple with it, of the farmer who grows rice in China. They say also that the housing problem in the slums of New York and Chicago is bound up with that of finding room for the overflowing populations of Belgium and Italy, India and Japan. In the early thirties when we were in the midst of a financial depression and a third of the people of our own country were underfed, badly housed and poorly clothed, we were confronted with the economic theory that it was no use trying to take care of our people unless at the same time we planned for the welfare of all the peoples of the world.

The crisis of our generation has been caused by the fact that all those problems have come to a head at one and the same time. It is an old adage that troubles never come singly. In a familiar line Shakespeare says, "When sorrows come, they come not single spies, but in battalions." The classic instance of course is that of God's good servant Job. But who is there that has not experienced in his own life or observed in the life of some one else, the sudden onslaught of many woes arriving together or in swift succession—ill health, loss of fortune, discharge from a job, betrayal by a trusted friend, ingratitude and even treason in one's own family, and who knows what other calamities, that fall upon one suddenly like an avalanche.

It happens to good people and to bad. When suffering comes upon a good man, he knows how to deal with it. He has his religion. When it comes upon a bad man, he is—to use the same word again—bewildered. He had said, or at least thought, "Behold I have sinned and no evil has come upon me." But his sins catch up with him, and as likely as not they all catch up with him at the same moment. He has been extravagant and profligate, unfaithful in his domestic duties and to his obligations as a citizen. The crash comes and all his sins come tumbling down upon his head. His creditors refuse him any more time of grace; his wife discovers his infidelity; his children are ashamed of him and perhaps disown him; his friends fall away; the government prosecutes him; those from whom he would seek help hide themselves from him; those to whom he looks for sympathy laugh at him. "One thing at a time," he cries. "I could stand one thing at a time." But life is not like that. The fates are merciless. Enemies, those whom he calls enemies, swarm in on him from all sides. He has to fight and to suffer or commit suicide. If he commits suicide his real sufferings begin.

Our present civilization is like that man. It has been an extravagant civilization, a profligate civilization. Like the prodigal in the Gospel the world has squandered its substance, material substance, moral and spiritual substance. The world has been going along without reference to God and with little or no concern for God's Commandments. Popes, priests, preachers, moralists have cried alarm repeatedly. Look back, for example, upon the Encyclicals that have issued from Rome since 1878 when Pope Leo XIII came to the throne, and through all the twenty-five years of his pontificate, and under his successors,

Pius X, Benedict XV, Pius XI, and the present Holy Father Pius XII. Their encyclical letters make a generous document of prophetic literature. In them you can see not only a brief abstract and chronicle of the evils of the day, but such warnings of impending doom as might have come from Isaias or Jeremias or Daniel.

The world paid little attention, went its way reckless, profligate, heedless. After all, said the secularists, we have science and education. Education will save us. We have a department of knowledge unknown to our ancestors, Sociology, which enables us to detect and diagnose disease in the social order, and to apply the cure. With the help of universal education, with the press and radio as well as the schools to disseminate knowledge we can reach great populations quickly and set them right if they are going wrong. We have passed out of the dark ages. We have light. We see our way. The priests tell us that we are "a wicked and adulterous generation." Perhaps we are, but in a wicked world there is more zest and adventure and excitement than in a pious world. And we are shrewd. We know how far we can go. When the time comes, we will halt and if need be turn back. As for those moralizings and melancholy prophecies in the papal encyclicals, repeated from the pulpit, in the religious press and over certain radio programs—we weary of them. This world is too big, too complicated, too busy, too progressive to be comprehended by those who got their education in ecclesiastical seminaries. Let priests and preachers confine themselves to homilies on the Gospel. What right or claim or competence have popes or prelates or common clergy to speak to us of economics as Leo did, or of Social Justice as Pius XI and Pius XII have done? Leave us alone. We can run this world.

So, they still pursue a form of education from which God is excluded. They still think they can construct a workable code of ethics with no assistance from religion. They still subscribe to the superstition that you can set the world right when it has gone wrong by enacting laws, more laws, more mountains of laws. Perhaps I may take a slight liberty with the poet's lines,

> Ill fares the land, to hastening ills a prey
> Where *laws accumulate,* and men decay.

They still place their reliance upon a sociology which spurns the assistance of theology, and a psychology, the science of the soul, which denies the existence of the soul. They are unfamiliar with the works of so profound a thinker as Christopher Dawson, whose writings are richly studded with such provocative passages as these:

"Never before in the history of the world has a civilization been so completely secularized, so confident in its own powers and so sufficient to itself as is our own. The crude and aggressive atheism of the Soviet State is but the logical culmination of a tendency that has characterized the general development of European civilization for the last century and a half. Indeed we may well ask if the toleration which is still shown to Christianity by the States of Western Europe is not due to the fact that religion is regarded by them as something politically negligible, and consequently whether it is not really more insulting to Christianity than the open hostility of the Bolsheviks."

And this: "European culture had already ceased to be Christian in the eighteenth century, but it still retained the inherited moral standards and values of a Christian civilization. And so it attempted to erect these standards into an independent system by providing a rational philosophic justification for them. But as Liberalism did not create these moral ideals, so, too, it cannot preserve them. It lives on the spiritual capital that it has inherited from Christian civilization, and as this is exhausted something else must come to take its place. Once society is launched on the path of secularization it cannot stop in the half-way house of Liberalism; it must go on to the bitter end, whether that end be Communism or some alternative type of 'totalitarian' secularism."

Is any one saying those things to the American people, any one except clergymen whose warnings are disregarded or discounted because it is thought that they have an ecclesiastical axe to grind?

The world has destroyed itself with worldly wisdom. It cannot resurrect itself with worldly wisdom. You may find that simple truth not only in the Gospels but in Mother Goose. When Humpty Dumpty falls off the wall, not all the king's horses and all the king's men can put him together again. When civilization topples and falls, not all the politicians nor all the professors can lift civilization up again. When the world is shattered no one can put the pieces together again except the One Who put them together in the first place, the One Who called the world into order out of Chaos. But the world must cry to Him to do it. When you leave out God—out of education, out of scientific progress, out of government and the affairs of nations, out of private and public life—all goes to wrack and ruin. If you will but call God back again, He will come and recreate the world.

Chapter 21

The Cause and the Cure

THE Church has been in this world a long long time. She can recall precedents in the past for all that happens today. She can say out of her own experience, "There is nothing new under the sun." Nothing that happens, good or bad, can surprise her. She has seen it all before. Nor has she grown old. "Ever ancient, ever new," describes her. She is neither senile nor moribund. Communists have a slogan, "Religion is opium." They must be thinking of Buddhism. Catholicism is not Buddhism, or any other system of spiritual stupefaction. The Church is alive, too terribly alive to suit her enemies.

I say she knows because she remembers. She says of one modern tyrant, "He reminds me of Augustus Caesar, in the first century"; of another, "He is repeating the mistake of Emperor Henry IV and of Frederick Barbarossa in the eleventh century"; of another, "He seems to be trying hard to be a Nero, a Caligula, a Peter the Great, or an Ivan the Terrible"; of another, "He overruns a continent, destroying as he goes like Attila in the fifth century, Mohammed in the seventh, Tamerlane in the thirteenth. They come; they go. I remain and I remember."

What the Catholic Church remembers she passes on to her popes, bishops, priests, to any one who cares to ask. It is, therefore, neither absurd nor arrogant of a Catholic to offer a cause and a cure for the evils of the world. He can dip into the memoirs of his Church and bring forth some samples of the wisdom she has accumulated. Of old when skeptics challenged our Savior to say by what authority He taught, He replied, "My teaching is not My own, but His Who sent Me." So, says the Catholic, "My remedy is not mine; I have it not out of my own head but from the experience of my Church."

Now, let us agree that the times are troubled. Some say that they are now more troubled than they ever were before. I don't think so myself, but I am not inclined to argue the point. Suffice it to say that the times are bad. The predicament in which civilization finds itself is serious. Say, if you will, that we are face to face with catastrophe. Say that the pillars that uphold the civilized world are tumbling, as the columns of the temple of Gaza fell at the hands of Samson; say, if you think it true, that the world will be destroyed entirely, "all our pomp of yesterday [will be] one with Nineveh and Tyre"; say that we have come once again to the days when noble cities, once centers of art and culture and commerce, lie devastated, and that the ruins of them shall lie forever choked in weeds as at Baalbek, or buried in the sands as at Babylon or Thebes. If you would pose as a prophet say that once again asps and basilisks will crawl over the stones of Rome as in the days of St. Gregory the Great, and, eight centuries later, of St. Catherine of Siena; say that the day may come, visualized if not prophesied by the British historian, when a traveler from "down under" will stand "in the midst of a vast solitude" in the heart of London; say with that other Britisher, a writer of fiction who fancied himself in the role of prophet in the 1920's, who used to reiterate that if we ever had one more war like that of 1914-18, civilization would be set back a thousand years; wrap yourself if you will in the mantle of Jonas; or cry, "Yet forty days and Nineveh shall be destroyed" and add "Yet forty days, or forty months and all the world—the world as we have known it—will be destroyed." Be as pessimistic as you please; let your diagnosis be as dismal and your outlook as despondent as you think the facts warrant. I still

make bold to say that the tottering world can be propped up
and made to stand; that even a ruined world can rise again. I
know—that is to say my Church knows and she has told me—
the secret of the Rise and Fall of Nations, the cause and the
cure of the collapse of civilizations.

The cause and the cure. You cannot know the cure unless
you know the cause. In the cause is the cure. Cause and cure
are the same, seen from different angles. The cause of collapse
is negative; something has been taken away. The cure is positive;
something must be replaced.

Now what is the cause of the sorry condition of the world?
The vogue of the moment is to say Communism. That answer
simplifies matters. The Jews of the Old Testament laid the sins
of the nation upon a scapegoat, and drove the beast out into the
wilderness. "The serpent did deceive me," said Adam. So today
we find it convenient to make of one man or one nation or one
institution the serpent and the devil all in one. But the world
was in a bad way before Communism arose, and it may be little
better when it will have disappeared. There are those who
borrow Voltaire's phrase if not Voltaire's idea and cry, "Blot
out the infamous thing." Voltaire's infamous thing was ecclesiasticism. But it wasn't ecclesiasticism that was endangering France.
It wasn't ecclesiasticism that brought on the Revolution. The
Revolutionists got rid of ecclesiastics but when the ecclesiastics
were out of the way, Robespierre and Danton had the stage to
themselves, and what a shambles they made of it!

Those who cry, "Blot out Fascism!" "Blot out Nazism!" "Blot
out Communism!," do not remember that. Tyrants are not a
cause but an effect. The cause that made them will make something worse. Get rid of Lenin and Stalin and you have Malen-
kovism or Bulganinism or what you will.

Well then, what *is* the cause of fascism and Communism?
Another easy "out" for those who like short cuts in thinking is
to say "Versailles," or Yalta or Potsdam or Geneva. I am no

apologist for wicked treaties, and compromising covenants. What is vindictive is foolish. "The wrath of man," says the Scripture, "worketh not the justice of God." They who tried to punish Germany, punished Europe. Versailles may have been the cause of Hitler and Hitler the cause of Stalin, but Stalinism existed before Versailles under the name of Leninism. Leninism was in operation before Versailles.

One view is that the present calamitous condition was caused by World War No. I and World War No. II and that the second was caused by the first. That theory is plausible. Wars make wars. The Thirty Years' War and the Hundred Years' War were not continuous wars so much as a succession of wars, one leading to another. Nevertheless World War No. I was not the cause of World War No. II, and the two wars were not the cause of our present troubles. Nor have we been harmed only by Yalta and other diplomatic capitulations. Philosophers make a distinction between cause and effect on the one hand and antecedent and consequent upon the other. The Scholastics have a principle, "The cause of the cause is the cause of what is caused." If, therefore, you seek the root cause of all our troubles you will have to go further back and deeper down.

The cause of the two wars and of the prevalent political chaos is a philosophy. The philosophy that is taught even now in America, and that has been taught for two generations in England and the United States no less than in Germany, is a philosophy from which God is excluded. The idea seems to be that if you introduce God into a philosophy it is not a philosophy but a theology. No more widely irrational idea ever took possession of the minds of learned men. Aristotle was no theologian, but he had a God in his philosophy. Socrates, the father of philosophy in the Western world, the philosopher *par excellence,* would have thought it madness to devise a philosophy without God. Not to run through all the philosophies that have been conceived and propagated since Socrates, be it said that not until recent times has any system of thought calling itself a philosophy rejected or ignored God.

When you get rid of God, you no longer have an Absolute. If there be no Absolute there remains only Relativity. The root cause of all the calamity that now exists and that threatens the death of civilization is the philosophy or the many philosophies of Relativism. I speak not of mathematical or astronomical relativity. What I have in mind as the cause of mental and moral anarchy is any and every system of thought which dispenses with the Absolute, that is, with God. We often say in sermons to the people, "No God, no Ten Commandments; no Ten Commandments, no moral law; no moral law, chaos." But that is only a hint of the harm that comes from getting rid of God.

I have read a philosopher who declares: "I will not hear of the Absolute. The very mention of the word Absolute annoys me." Very well then, let us say there is no Absolute. All is relative. Truth is relative. Justice is relative. Right is relative. If there is no Absolute, there is no Universal. What was true in the time of Christ and in Palestine need not be true here and now in America. What seemed good to Moses for his people in the wilderness is not good for our people in a sophisticated urban civilization. No code of morals adapted to the temperate zone is good in the tropics. What is right and good and true and beautiful in England or the United States need not be good in Germany or Russia, or China, or India.

What next? If there be no Absolute Truth, Right, Justice, the door is wide open to such a philosopher as Thomas Hobbes who says "Justice is what the State says it is." If Justice is what the State says it is, Truth is what the State says it is, and Right and Virtue, Morality, Patriotism; everything is what the State says it is.

But from the day when Jesus Christ stood before Pilate and Herod, from the day and long before that, when the Prophets of Israel confronted a recalcitrant people and were stoned to death, all saints and martyrs have refused to accept the idea that what the State says is true is true indeed; that the State can make or unmake right or wrong; that the State can create or destroy morality with an edict; that the State can declare an unjust war just; that the State can put its official stamp upon fanaticism and make it patriotism; that the State can permit or abolish religion at will, or say which religion shall be tolerated and which be outlawed; that the State in brief can take possession of the whole man body and soul; that the State can proclaim its own Absolute Sovereignty with the words: "Nothing above the State; nothing beyond the State; nothing outside the State."

This blasphemy is the essence of Fascism, Nazism, Communism; ultimately, philosphically, they are one and the same. They add up to this: There is no Absolute God; the only Absolute is the State.

The final and supreme result of an atheistic philosophy is that when you get rid of the Absolute God you clear the way not only for the Absolute State, but for the Absolute man. When the Roman religion was in decay and the idea of a supreme God waned, the Emperor had himself declared God. Caesar Augustus was god. Nero was god. Caligula was god. The early Christians were slaughtered because they would not offer incense to the emperor-god.

"If there were no God we should have to create one," said Voltaire. He might have worded it differently. When the philosophers say there is no God, the people make to themselves a god. When the people make their own god, it is a monster, a god of blood and passion, a fiery fanatical god; a god who flies easily and frequently into a frenzy; a ruthless, bloodthirsty god, a maniac god issuing crazy commands, a threatening god breathing fire like Moloch; a god who dreams and plans to subdue the whole world and make of all men his footstool.

That's the kind of god you get when you reject the One True Absolute God. For mankind must have and will have a god, some kind of god. If the philosophers don't know that, they don't know man; and how can one be a philosopher if one doesn't know human nature?

Yet almost every modern philosophy denies God or ignores God. They who say that there is not in their philosophy a place for an Absolute God, are the makers of Lenin and Stalin and Hitler; they with their philosophy are cause of chaos. It rejoices them to see the people and those who pretend to explain affairs to the people focusing attention upon some scapegoat. The guilty ones remain unnoticed in the general confusion.

Let us repeat: The cause behind the cause of Fascism, Nazism and Communism, and of all the evils that flow from those poisoned sources, is Atheism. The cure is to bring back God, the Ultimate Absolute Truth, Justice, Right. Do that and you shall have a basis upon which to reconstruct even this tottering civilization.

Chapter 22

Americanism in Theology

THERE is no essential reason to deny the right of Americans to put their stamp upon world Catholicism. We must not repeat the mistake implied if not expressed in Hilaire Belloc's slogan, "Europe is the Faith and the Faith is Europe." Still less are we to claim that America is the faith and the faith is America. William T. Stead some forty or fifty years ago sponsored a movement for what he called "the Americanization of the World." It is odd, perhaps unique, that an Englishman should use that phrase with anything but contempt and revulsion. But no wise American would care to see the world Americanized. Still less would he care to see the Church Americanized. But neither should it be Latinized or Gallicized or Germanized. It is very well for the French to speak proudly of *la patrie* as "the eldest daughter of the Church" and to boast of what God has done for all mankind by means of the French, *gesta Dei per Francos*. But they must not try to convey the impression that "there is no nation that hath its God so nigh to it" as France. They might do well to recall St. Augustine's rejection of the idea—the very curious idea, indeed—apparently broached by some North African Latins in Carthage and Hippo, that God had redeemed Africa and no other land.

It is of the genius of the Church to embody within herself some of the characteristics of all peoples. "Spiritually we are Semites" is a phrase of the Pope's which has been much quoted of late. We were in the beginning predominantly Semitic, and the Semitic influence remains after nineteen centuries. But there is equally evident in the constitution of the Church the Byzantine and the Greco-Roman influence. The outstanding achievement of St. Paul was to fuse the Semitic with the Greek and Latin, the East and the West. He would have been the first to deny that "never the twain shall meet."

Every living body assimilates into itself nutriment from its surroundings. A man may live for part of his life in the temperate zone and take his sustenance from the foods proper to that zone. He may move to the tropics or to the arctic and learn to subsist on a very different diet. Indeed man is the most adaptable of animals. In him is found above all others "adaptation to environment." But no matter what he absorbs, he remains the same man.

Now, this power of assuming and assimilating various elements is found in the Church as in no other organism. Missionaries do wisely when they make no attempt to tear up and cast away all the native customs which they find among prospective converts, but rather to graft Catholic doctrine and Catholic practice upon the tree they find already planted and growing. The Incas and the Aztecs, for example, were not called upon to become Spanish under penalty of remaining forever pagan. The Slavic peoples, who came late into the Church, brought with them the characteristics of their race. The "Italians" of post-invasion days introduced the customs of the Goths and the Lombards. Much may be detected by ethnologists that is peculiarly Gaelic in the actual practice of the Catholic religion in Scotland and Ireland. Certain African or Asiatic idiosyncrasies remain when converts are made in Uganda and Ceylon.

But this is all too obvious. The only question is: Should Catholics in the United States of America alone be forbidden to retain their racial idiosyncrasies, their political preferences, their national customs? "I heard you had become a Catholic," said someone to a convert who had given a lecture on St. Patrick, "but I didn't know you had become an Irishman." Must a Yankee indeed first become Irish before he can be a Catholic?

As of racial, so of political traits. Should the American convert be taught in the catechism that he must accept monarchy and repudiate democracy before he can come into the fold? As I was writing these sentences, there came into my mind a suspicion that all this had been said long ago, that it had been woven into my thinking and that now after many years I was giving it off at if it were my discovery. So I looked up Archbishop John Ireland's Introduction to *The Life of Father Hecker* by Father Walter Elliott, and this is what I found:

"It is clear that countries and peoples have each their peculiar needs and aspirations as they have their peculiar environments, and that, if we would enter into souls and control them, we must deal with them according to their conditions. The ideal line of conduct for the priest in Assyria will be out of all measure in Mexico or Minnesota, and I doubt not that one doing fairly well in Minnesota would by similar methods set things sadly astray in Leinster or Bavaria. The Savior prescribed timeliness in pastoral caring. The master of the house, He said, 'bringeth forth out of his treasury new things and old,' as there is demand for one kind or the other. The apostles of nations, from Paul before the Areopagus to Patrick upon the summit of Tara, followed no different principle."

The rule works both ways. If a priest from Minnesota goes back to Cork or Dublin, he must not attempt to make "Yankees" of the folks in the old country, and the priest from Ireland or Poland or France or Germany, working in America, should not look upon the members of his flock as merely transplanted Europeans. When the French in Canada cry *"Notre langue, notre foi,"* it is very well if they mean that they have a right to their language as to their faith. But when they move out of "New France" into New England, they should not indoctrinate their children with the idea that to speak English is to lose the faith.

Perhaps the most extreme example of the desirability of keeping racial characteristics in mind when presenting the faith to those who have it not is the suggestion of Charles de Foucauld, onetime soldier in France, later hermit in Morocco, who held that it would be well to ease up on preaching and emphasize the mystical and eremitical element of religion if we are to appeal to the Moslems. That theory may meet opposition on scriptural grounds: "Go . . . preach" and "Faith cometh by hearing." But on the other hand it may be contended that among a people given to mysticism, contemplation should be especially emphasized. Be that as it may, if the Moslems have remained adamant in their resistance to preaching and we can win them to the gospel by living amongst them as hermits, with little other apologetic, it may be that de Foucauld has made a significant suggestion.

At any rate Catholics of any race should hesitate to inflict their ethnic and political idiosyncrasies upon those who are not of their blood and tradition. Canon Jacques Leclercq in a witty passage of his *Dialogue de l'Homme et de Dieu* says: "All Christian peoples consider themselves superior, and in proportion as their Christian tradition is strong they seek to demonstrate an especial bond between themselves and Christ. The French think that God cannot do without them. The Germans, the Italians, the English, have similar convictions. To express the idea that a man seems to be a good fellow, no better praise can be found than to say, 'He is like one of ourselves.' " Leclercq adds with delicious French *malice*, "The Esquimaux think the same, and so do we."

The first Paulists were to the American manner born. They had accumulated experience on missions in many States and they had come to the conclusion that if the faith is to flourish in America, those who preach it must not force converts into a racial and political mold other than their own. Father Hecker said it in a sentence: "So far as is compatible with faith and piety I am for accepting the American civilization with its uses and customs; the character and spirit of our people and their institutions must find themselves at home in our Church as those of other nations have done."

It may not be too much to say that the thriving condition of the Church in the United States today is due in large degree to the acceptance of that principle. Such, by the way, is really all there is to "Americanism." At least that is all that "Americanism" meant in America.

Chapter 23

Politics in Religion: Religion in Politics

IN almost every platform lecture, radio address and after-dinner speech nowadays; in the more serious kind of magazine article and in a multitude of books, occurs the statement, or its equivalent, "We live in a world of confusion." True. So obviously true that it seems silly to say it. But there are various kinds of confusion, and the most fundamental kind is seldom so much as mentioned. I mean mental confusion, confusion in the realm of reasoning. The prevalent political confusion and moral confusion would clear away promptly if men would only think straight. Of course there are persons who don't want to think. They seem to say, "Don't ask me to think. Don't let me think." But most men would like to think if they could. The heart of man is generally in the right place but his thinking apparatus is—as the Russians say—"Kapoot," "out of order." Dr. Nicholas Murray Butler years ago made a significant speech on "Thinking as a Lost Art." Alexander Pope three hundred years earlier had put it in one of his unforgettable rhymed couplets:

> How few think justly of the thinking few.
> How many never think who think they do.

Not three hundred but three thousand years earlier, the prophet Jeremias said what the professor and the poet were to say, and said it more eloquently: "With desolation is all the world made desolate because no man thinketh."

Enough of that. It is a tempting theme but it is not now my

purpose to develop it. What I have in mind is that one evidence of lame and impotent thinking is the instantaneous reaction to the title of this chapter, "Religion in Politics, Politics in Religion." "Keep those things apart," people say; "Separate them as day from night. No, not that, for after all there is a twilight in which night and day meet and mingle. Separate religion and politics with the impassable abyss which, as our father Abraham told Dives, separates Heaven from hell." Which of the two, Religion or Politics, corresponds to Heaven and which to Hell, seems to be a matter of debate. In Russia they say that religion is hell. In America we profess to believe that politics is more likely to be of the pit. But oddly enough, both in the U.S.S.R. and in the U.S.A., there is wide agreement that religion and politics must be kept as far apart as God and Satan.

But from the beginning of the world until now there has never been a kingdom, an empire, a state, a city, or any form of political society from which religion was excluded. It has never been done because it cannot be done. It has been attempted; it has been momentarily and partially accomplished. But you can no more take religion out of a State and keep it out than you can take hydrogen, oxygen, and nitrogen out of the air and keep them out. You can indeed make a vacuum—a small vacuum in a laboratory—but when you produce a vacuum, Nature summons all her force to destroy it. So, you can take religion out of a State, but Nature—human nature—will put it back again. The maddest of all psychological blunders is to imagine that religion is something unnatural imposed upon man by priestcraft, and that therefore it must be kept out of the more important affairs of men. If some atheistic tyrant were bold enough and strong enough to kill all priests and lay all temples of religion flat to the ground, religion would spout anew from the earth, as the grass and the grains and the flowers grow again on a battlefield that has been made a desert by shot and shell and poison gas. Religion comes down from above but also it comes out of the soil, out of the blood and bone of man, out of his heart and mind and soul. To take religion out of human life would have the same effect as taking the elements out of the atmosphere.

Another mistake of the opponents of religion is that they recognize no distinction between good and bad, true and false religion. Atheists in general reject all religion because some religion is vile. It is like rejecting all food because some food is poison; or like the logic of the man who, reading that people are killed by stepping on a cake of soap in a bath tub, resolved never again to use soap and never to get into a tub; or of the woman who reads that thousands of accidents take place in the kitchen and vows never to set foot in a kitchen. Silly? Of course, but no sillier than a great deal of what passes for thinking in these irrational times. Are there not persons who don't go to Church because some who go to Church are hypocrites? "I don't make my Easter duty," said one man to me (a big man in the business world), "because the last time I went to Holy Communion I saw at the Altar rail people who owe me money and don't pay." The logic is that of the Chinaman who commits suicide on the door step of the one who has done him a wrong. I have also met college students who gave up religion because they had read in H. G. Wells or Grant Allen or in James G. Frazer that savages believe in a savage god. Does any Church ask a civilized man to believe in a savage god? Is there not a civilized God for civilized people? If they don't like the god of Senegambia, or for that matter the top-hat god, the roll-top desk swivel-chair god in "Green Pastures," what about the God of Thomas Aquinas or of St. Augustine? What about the God of Jesus Christ? The silliest reasoning, the wildest logic seems to suffice the man who doesn't want to go to Church, as it does the man who doesn't want to take a bath or go to bed.

In getting rid of God, the atheists, especially the Soviet atheists of Moscow, make a god of the people or as they say, the prole- tariat. But the people can be as cruel as any fabulous god. "The people, Sir, is a great beast," said Alexander Hamilton. Great beast indeed, great monster, like the people in the courtyard of the Pretorium of Pilate who howled like maniacs for the release of a murderer and the crucifixion of Christ. But shall we therefore say that the people, all the people all the time is a great beast? Where will such wild logic lead us?

I am no professional apologist for politics and still less for politicians. But I think it only fair to say that the science and the art of politics have been the victims of crooked thinking in the same way, if not to the same degree, as religion. Some men—shall I say most men—when they say "politics" have in mind degraded politics, corrupt politics.

But what is politics? Let's have a definition. Not a sarcastic definition, a cynical or a jocose definition. Venom aside and jesting aside, what is politics? Politics, says the dictionary, is "the science which treats of the principles of civil government and the conduct of state affairs in the interest of peace, prosperity, and safety." And again: Politics is "that branch of ethics which deals with the relation and duties of States or social organizations." Evidently there is nothing ignoble or debased or shameful about that kind of politics. Of course you may also find in the dictionaries secondary definitions of politics, "partisanship," "factional rivalries," "intrigues," "wire-pulling," "trickery." But it is a mistake in logic and an unfair procedure to lump good politics with bad and condemn all politics.

Politics is not only a branch of life. It is an indispensable requisite for the welfare of the human race. Were there no politics there would be anarchy. American Communists when confronted with the cruelties of the Soviet State sometimes explain that these cruelties are temporary and that the time will come when the State can afford to dispense with cruelty and that indeed the ultimate aim of Communism is the abolition of the State. Oddly enough, the same objective was visualized by Friedrich Nietzsche, forerunner of Nazism. He held that all States and all governments are tyrants and must finally be done away with. When there is no State there will be no politics and no politicians, but when there is no State there will also be anarchy.

Putting aside fallacious and unreasonable notions of politics and of religion, it becomes plain that the greatest boon to the human race, at any time and especially in the present crisis would be the co-operation of pure politics and right religion. What ails the world is the elimination of religion from politics. Strange that well disposed men and women cannot see that fact. A preacher in the pulpit says to the congregation: "When you leave the Church take your religion with you. Don't leave it in the pew. Take it into your home, into the kitchen, into the bedroom, into all your family life and social life. Take religion with you when you go to work. You will need it in the office, in the factory, in the mine and the mill more than you need it in Church. Take religion with you when you go to a place of entertainment. If there is an incongruity between your religion and your entertainment, seek some other entertainment in which your religion, your conscience, the welfare of your soul, will be safeguarded. And so on. And so on. A sermon like that will be praised as "Practical" and "Sensible."

But shall we then say to a man whose vocation is politics: "Leave your religion in Church or at home when you go to the council chamber or the caucus, to parliament or to congress? It is done indeed. There are Sabbath Day saints who are week day villains. But the cure for that condition is not to separate religion and politics but to combine them. It is not too much to say that the present sad condition of the world has come to pass because of the secularization of politics. Politicians of the baser type, especially since the French Revolution, have insisted that God be kept out of all affairs of State. "Let us settle our problems," they say, "make our plans and direct our government without reference to God."

Those who say such things are not aware of the implication

of what they say. If you leave out God, you leave out justice and right and truth. It cannot be repeated too often—though the more we repeat it the less some people seem to understand—God *is* Justice, God *is* Right and Truth. If you leave God out of politics, out of government, out of treaties and covenants and all political pacts, you leave out Truth and Righteousness and Mercy; you have remaining only expediency, selfish interest, international rivalries. If you leave out God you leave out all chance for lasting peace. There is no hope for peace in the midst of natural antipathies unless you turn to the supernatural. The Ultimate Absolute Supernatural is God.

Those may seem to be, and they are, profound metaphysical statements and perhaps for that reason politicians have not grasped them. But politicians worthy to be called statesmen have not ignored them. George Washington declared, "Reason and experience both forbid us to expect that national morality can prevail in exclusion of religious principles." Thomas Jefferson did not leave God out of the Declaration of Independence. All men, he says, have been endowed by their Creator with certain rights. These rights were begotten not of flesh and blood, not of the will of man, but of God. If the rights of man are from man, man can take them away. If they are the gift of the State, the State can withhold the gift or demand it back. But if the rights of man are of God, no man and no State can alienate them.

Treaties of peace especially must be negotiated and ratified in the name of God. In earlier days all great covenants commenced with the phrase, *"In Nomine Domini: Amen."* "In the Name of the Lord: So be it." I will venture further. War must be declared and waged, if at all, in the Name of God. If men do not dare to call God to witness the justice of a war, it is no just war for them. To leave God out of war is to admit the Godlessness of war. St. Thomas Aquinas lays down as one of the requisites of a just war that it must be conducted in the spirit of justice and love. He justifies war only on condition that it be an instrument in the hand of man to do the will of God. Today, that high and holy doctrine is considered ridiculous or impossible. But it remains true that if a war cannot be justified in the eyes of God it is not just. To declare war or to participate in a war without reference to God is as sacrilegious as to attempt to conduct any political function without the sanction and the help of religion.

In peace, in war, in all the relationships of man with man, nation with nation, we must remain under the aegis of God, or we shall perish.

Chapter 24

Communism: Academic and Actual

ONE of the American fliers, released from Soviet China after years of imprisonment and torture, reported that some of the indignities inflicted upon him were such as he would not care to describe. There is, I imagine, great significance beneath that not too cryptic statement. Those who have carefully followed the course of Communism will be able, perhaps, to fill in the details that were so discreetly and mercifully concealed by the airman.

There are punishments which, though cruel, are in the line of nature. There are others that are unnatural, sadistic, and others still that can be described only by a word that has for most people lost its original meaning—fiendish. The "foul fiend," as the medieval man called Satan, was no brute. He had been before his fall highly intelligent, and so he remained. He can apply his knowledge to the torture of man. But in none of the tortures of hell hitherto described in theology or in poetry is there evidence that Satan possessed and utilized what we call modern science. What he didn't know he couldn't utilize.

But now we have the monstrous phenomenon of men with the primitive instincts of savages making use of the most recent physiology and psychology to intensify the torture of their prisoners. The cavemen had no such knowledge, nor had the inventors of the rack, the Catherine-wheel, the Iron Virgin and other such ingenious devices. Since the beginning of the age of enlightenment we may have been led to believe that we had come to the end, or at least the beginning of the end of man's inhumanity to man. Obviously we have not. Communism—Russian, Chinese, Korean, and indeed Middle European—has added something new to produce tortures hitherto unknown.

Some of the intellectuals, characteristically slow to detect what goes on in the world of realism, seem unaware of the brutishness, the savagery, the fiendishness of Communist torture. Not long ago I heard a professor say, "After all, Communism and Christianity have essentially the same philosophy." I could not but wonder in what ivory tower he had taken refuge from reality during the last two or three decades. It is, or should be, incredible that an intelligent person could completely insulate himself from life and from matters of common knowledge.

The absent-minded professor of an older vintage of joke books used to be good for a laugh. We had thought the species extinct. Of "Mr. Chips" (who by the way was not so naive as he seemed) we had been accustomed to say, like Daniel Webster to the veterans of the Revolution, "You have come down to us from a former generation." But it seems there are still extant certain facsimiles of Mr. Chips, escapees from the academic cloister, who think of Communism as a philanthropic and humanitarian philosophy. The late Irwin Edman once wrote of a taxicab driver who gave him a definition of philosophy—"intensified common sense." Some scholars I have met or have read seem to make of philosophy intensified nonsense.

The fact is, of course, that there is not now and that there has not been since 1918 a philosophical, not to say a theological, Communism. The brutish slaughter of the Tsar, his wife and family, the Kronstadt incident, the "liquidation," that is to say the wholesale murder of the Kulaks, the enslavement of scores of millions of workers, have put an end to the naive belief in an academic Communism.

The intellectual is not alone in being blind to what is going on in the world. Judging from some of the statements of presidents and premiers, senators, members of Congress and of

Parliament, justices of the Supreme Court (some of them), editors of some newspapers and magazines, authors and publishers of certain books, writers of a good many syndicated columns, and other assorted practitioners of the art of publicity and propaganda, they do not know the time of day.

There is a Scripture text that of late comes to the suface of my consciousness a dozen times a day: "Jerusalem, Jerusalem, if thou hadst but known and that in this thy day the things that are to thy peace, but now they are hidden from thy eyes. For the days shall come upon thee and thy enemies shall . . . beat thee flat to the ground . . . because thou hast not known the time of thy visitation." For "Jerusalem" substitute "America" or even "The Western World" and the warning is up to date, indeed up to the moment.

Perhaps the significant remark of the American flier that he would not care to describe the kind of torture to which the Communists subjected him, may serve as an illumination to theorists who have been living mentally on some transcendental planet quite out of touch with this nether world.

Chapter 25

Loyalty

The Church must often contradict the world. The world's standards are graded down to meet the convenience of the morally and spiritually mediocre. But the Church keeps her sights high. "Christ," some one has said, "invariably took the loftiest view of the capacity of human nature"; and the Church follows her Master. So it happens that there is a constant feud between the standards of the Christian and those of the worldly-minded. Many examples could be cited, but one will suffice. The matter of sins of the flesh. The Church teaches that carnal desire—not to say carnal action—can be a mortal sin. "Whosoever shall look upon a woman to lust after her," says our Savior, "has already committed adultery with her in his heart." The world in general repudiates that teaching as puritanical. Indeed—to judge from novels, plays, musical comedies, women's dress at the beach, in the ballroom and even on the street, the world in general considers stimulants to sexual excitement permissible and desirable.

As with impurity and immodesty that incites to impurity, so with a thousand other matters. The Church and the world do not (to borrow the wishy washy phrase) see eye to eye. But there is one virtue upon which the Church and the World, religion and irreligion agree—loyalty is always, everywhere and by everybody considered paramount. The savage is loyal to the taboos of his tribe; the Arab is loyal to the stranger who has eaten salt at his table; the criminal has a code which he would die rather than violate; the member of a secret society is loyal to his oath; the Ku Klux Klansman to what he calls racial and religious purity. The white man in some Southern states surrounded and, as he thinks, in danger of being engulfed by the blacks, holds to the principle of "white supremacy"; the aristocrat makes a last ditch stand against the democratization of society; the West Pointer from cadet to five star general upholds the code of "an officer and a gentleman." The patriot is loyal to his country, and when patriotism is unenlightened—to his country right or wrong.

So it goes from top to bottom, saints and sinners, heroes and criminals, among all peoples and in all classes of society "loyalty" is held to be the first of virtues. Evidently much that passes for loyalty is not a virtue at all. As often as not loyalty is misguided, perverted, distorted. In such cases it can lead to great injustice. In John Galsworthy's play, *Loyalties,* an army captain, in a tight spot as a result of gambling and other dissipation steals from a wealthy Jew at a house party. The victim is at first inclined to overlook the theft, but stung by insults to his people, blurts out "my race was old when you were all savages," and decides to bring the matter to the courts. Faced with a scandal, the entire group, though aware that the captain is the culprit, stand by him. A general is loyal and upholds the army's *esprit de corps;* the captain's wife clings to him as do the host and hostess. They are one and all "loyal" after their fashion to their race and to the traditions of the aristocracy. They doubtless considered themselves Christians but in the circumstances they would do injustice and if necessary commit perjury. Even the "good pagan" motto *Fiat justitia ruat coelum* ("let justice be done though the heavens fall") would not appeal to them. It all makes for tense drama and it presents, to those who are not well-grounded in ethics, a moral problem. It really highlights the fact that so-called loyalty may not be a virtue but a vice. No virtue is a virtue unless, as the Scholastics say, it is "well-ordered."

The early Christians became martyrs in defense of the

principle that between one loyalty and another one must make
the proper choice. Otherwise the highest heroism becomes the
basest cowardice. Under the Caesars loyalty to the State was
held to be above all others. The martyrs said, "We must obey
God rather than man," and they died by millions in defense of
that, quite obvious to us, fact. When the Romans identified God
and the State—even God and the Caesar—the followers of
Jesus, simple people almost all, were not beguiled. Many centuries later, St. Thomas More and St. John Fisher came face to
face with a similar problem, the theory that loyalty to the State
is antecedent to loyalty to the Church and patriotism to religion.
The Chancellor of the realm and the bishop, unlike the majority
of the laity and the hierarchy, could no more be tricked by a
fallacy than frightened by the threat of the ax. There are those
who in our own day, in violation of truth and logic contrast
"American Freedom" and "Catholic Power," and repeat the doctrine—heretical and immoral—that the State, in all things, even
religion and education, takes precedence over the Church, and
indeed over the individual conscience. The American Republic
has no more right than the Roman Empire or the British Com-
monwealth to coerce conscience. As for Catholics, we are as loyal
as anyone to the American government and to authentic American traditions, but if and when occasion demands we shall insist
that religious conviction and conscience are not to be subordi-
nated to law which may be enacted today and abrogated in a
decade or a generation. Our loyalties are "well-ordered." We
say of our Church what St. Paul said of his Gospel: it is "not
according to man, neither did I receive it of man, nor did I
learn it but by the revelation of Jesus Christ."

The most thrilling stories of loyalty are not in the drama or
in secular history but in the Bible. One might even say that the
Bible is primarily a record of magnificent loyalties. The Jews,
beset on all sides by idolatry and heathenish immorality in Palestine, Egypt, Babylon, are loyal to the one only God, and (though

like ourselves with varying degrees of tenacity) to the Decalogue. In the Gospels loyalty reaches its climax. Perhaps the supreme example after that of Christ Himself is St. Paul. With what has seemed to some a lack of humility, he is absolutely sure of himself. He seems not to have learned—or perhaps it is truer to say that he had thoroughly learned—a lesson from the fall of St. Peter and the other apostles who said, "We will go to death with Thee," but ran away from Jesus when the crisis came. Not too much must be made of that one breakdown in loyalty. James and John, being asked by the Lord, "Can you drink the chalice whereof I shall drink?" answered "We can," and they did.

Theirs was a confident kind of religion. We could have more of it nowadays. Those who think that a Christian must meet the world or the devil in an apologetic way, making excuses when he falls into sin, have failed to grasp the supremacy of loyalty in the religion of the One who stood silent but in complete control of the situation, before Pilate and Herod and the mob. Ours in not a timid, bashful, timorous religion. We don't apologize to the world for existing. We don't capitulate to the flesh like the poor degenerate who said in the attempt to hide his shame behind a barrier of wit, "The best way to overcome a temptation is to yield to it." We don't even strike our colors to the devil. I once heard a priest criticized for being an "inveterate challenger." The critic seemed to forget that we have all been challengers since our baptism. "Do you renounce Satan?" "I do renounce him." "And all his works?" "I do renounce them." "And all his pomps?" "I do renounce them." We throw down the gauntlet to the power of evil. If and when he picks it up (he always does) and comes at us full force, we don't cringe or quail. We pray "God have mercy on me," but we never cry "Satan take pity on me."

When the Lord God said to Satan, "Hast thou considered my servant Job, that there is none like him in the earth, a man simple and upright and fearing God and avoiding evil and still keeping his innocence" it was, to use a modern term, a vote of confidence in Job. Satan accepted the challenge, and the ensuing conflict between the "simple innocent" man and the master of all evil is not only classic in literature—but an example to those who think that religion is for cowards.

But of all "challengers" we may perhaps select St. Paul. I know of no more confident utterance in the history of the conflict of man with evil than that in the eighth chapter of his epistle to the Romans: "Who then shall separate us from the love of Christ? Shall tribulation? or distress? or famine? or nakedness? or persecution? or the sword?" He answers, "I am sure that neither death nor life, nor angels, nor principalities, nor powers, nor things present nor things to come, nor might, nor height, nor depth nor any other creature shall be able to separate us from the love of God which is in Christ Jesus our Lord." But best of all is the aftermath, "I have fought the good fight, I have finished my course, I have kept the faith." He was as good as his word. I have heard him called a braggadocio. The pious Christian— pious in a timid way—who made that remark did not know the meaning of the epithet he was using. A braggadocio is one who boasts and runs. There was no power on earth that could make St. Paul run away. Forty young men took oath that they would not eat or drink or sleep until they had killed him. They may have died of hunger and thirst and insomnia. But their oath didn't feaze him. A braggadocio doesn't make good. St. Paul made good. It has often been said that the early Christians destroyed the Empire simply by submitting. The statement is true in the sense in which it is made.

But when St. Paul bends his neck to the sword, or a martyr in the arena faces the wild beasts on the sand and 40,000 or 80,000 other "wild beasts" in the benches of the amphitheatre, and testifies to Christ, it seems a misuse of words to speak of that tremendous challenge as "submission." "Come fire and cross, come conflict with wild beasts, come rending of the whole body," said St. Ignatius of Antioch, "only may they aid me in attuning to the love of Jesus Christ . . ." and St. Polycarp: "Four and eighty years have I served Him and He never did me harm. Why should I now desert Him in my old age." The annals of the martyrs ancient and modern are filled with such confident declarations. We need not go to Plutarch's *Viri Romae* for examples of loyalty. The noblest form of loyalty is religion.

Perhaps—indeed in my mind there is no "perhaps"—we Christians with our faint and all but washed-out image of primitive Christianity don't make more headway in converting the world because the note of challenge has gone out of our faith. We capitulate, or at least compromise, too easily with the world the flesh and the devil. What we need is loyalty.

Chapter 26

World Unity I

IT WOULD seem that not until recent years have we become accustomed to the demand for World Unity. But the idea and the
hope, if not the demand and expectation, are not new. As early
as 1774 Oliver Goldsmith wrote an essay on *National Prejudices,*
in which occurs a passage that might have come from the lips
of a "One Worlder" of today: "Among all the famous sayings of
antiquity, there is none that does greater honour to the author,
or affords greater pleasure to the reader than that of the old
philosopher, who, being asked what countryman he was, replied,
that he was a citizen of the world. How few are there to be
found in modern times who can say the same. We are now
become so much Englishmen, Frenchmen, Dutchmen, Spaniards,
or Germans, that we are no longer citizens of the world; general
inhabitants of the globe, or members of that grand society which
comprehends the whole human kind."

In our own country just before the Civil War the enthusiastic
(shall we say over-enthusiastic?) abolitionist William Lloyd
Garrison had a slogan, "My country is the world, my countrymen
are all mankind." Orestes Brownson, rare example of a deep
thinker who was also an agitator, said in a lecture at Brook
Farm, "We must have no party but mankind." George Curtis
asked, "Do you think that will ever happen?" Brownson replied,
"Perhaps; after such a great war as the world has not yet wit-
nessed, from which the heart recoils with horror." That was

not only before our two World Wars, but some twenty years before the North-South conflict.

It would be a simple matter to cite a dozen or a hundred other such expressions of the laudable sentiment of world brotherhood. Perhaps some one has made an anthology of them. But let us have only one more, the most familiar of all, that of Tennyson who in "Locksley Hall" (for its greater part a bitter poem) anticipates the happy outcome of what the Founding Fathers of the American Republic called "the interminable and insensate wars of Europe."

For I dipt into the future, far as human eye could see,
Saw the Vision of the world, and all the wonder that would be;
Saw the heavens fill with commerce, argosies of magic sails,
Pilots of the purple twilight, dropping down with costly bales;
Heard the heavens fill with shouting, and there rain'd a ghastly dew
From the nations' airy navies grappling in the central blue;
Far along the world-wide whisper of the south-wind rushing warm,
With the standards of the peoples plunging thro' the thunder-storm
Till the war-drum throbb'd no longer, and the battle-flags were furl'd
In the Parliament of man, the Federation of the world.
There the common sense of most shall hold a fretful realm in awe,
And the kindly earth shall slumber, lapt in universal law.

The poet was obviously something of a prophet at least in regard to "airy navies grappling in the central blue," "the heavens filled with shouting," "rained a ghastly dew." Who is there who would not rejoice to see the fulfillment of the pleasanter part of the prediction, "the parliament of man, the federation of the world"? No humanitarian, no one who has any place high or low with Abou Ben Adhem on the angel's list of those who love their fellow man, would ridicule the idea of world unity or do anything to delay its coming. But the most fervent idealist must have at least a trace of realism in his character. At least we must have a clear statement of what kind of unity we are to seek.

Is it to be political, military, legislative, economic, social, ideological, or all of these? Its advocates do not specify. Still less do they make it clear whether they think a moral and spiritual unity essential. Few, if any of them even so much as mention religious unity. Hilaire Belloc used to say that unless there is cultural unity (of course religion is part of "culture") we had better remain apart. That proposition is perhaps debatable, but if so it should be debated not ignored. But it would seem that the advocates of world union consider religious unity not only unattainable but undesirable. They seem to consider Christ's prayer "that they may be one, O Heavenly Father as Thou and I are one" visionary. They are impatient with those of us who ask for clarification upon that point. We consider God as, among many other things, the Principle of Unity. From Him we all come; to Him we all return. In Him, if at all, we are to be united. Especially we think of God incarnate in man, Jesus Christ. But even yet, a dozen years after the inauguration of the United Nations He has not been welcomed to the Assembly or the Council. The Founder of our civilization is not quoted or even officially referred to. Some time ago at Town Hall, New York, in a debate on the method of obtaining peace among men, the name of Jesus was not mentioned until 52 of the 60 minutes allotted to discussion had passed—and when His Name was finally presented the result was laughter!

Perhaps we Christians are partly responsible for the creation of the impasse in the U.N. We made a similar decision some 1900 years ago. Christ would have been welcome to a pedestal in the Roman Pantheon. Indeed there was one Emperor who actually installed a statue of Jesus alongside those of Mars, Bacchus, Diana, Venus, Isis, Osiris, and the rest. But the early Christians were not placated. "The gods of the gentiles are demons," they said, quoting the Hebrew prophets. For thousands of years the Jews had upheld the principle of only One God, and it would have been no less than apostasy if Christians, who are spiritually and theologically continuators of Judaism, were to abandon the primary principle of Judaism. We could indeed fraternize with Mohammedans who repeat with the Jews "The Lord your God is one God." But can we, in the interests of world unity pretend to coalesce with polytheism?

Still more important is the question: shall we pretend to see no difficulty, no immorality, in sitting down with those who deny God altogether? What part hath Christ with Belial? What part hath God with anti-God? If we do sit down to negotiate, shall we proceed without reference to our God and our religion? Must we pretend to believe that deference to God is an impertinence in negotiations that are to determine the future of the world and the fate of mankind? Must we in the name of tolerance be guilty of moral cowardice and of the intellectual crime of abandoning our first principle? God is our First Principle.

In the interest of unity within the Greco-Roman Empire pagans insisted that Christianity should amalgamate with the religion of the State. To them the alternative Diana or Christ was meaningless. They suggested Diana *and* Christ. Must we now say not God *or* no God, but God *and* no God? Is not that the suicide of thought?

If those to whom God is not a Reality but a name or a convention—sometimes a convenience and at other times a nuisance —accuse us of intolerance because we insist that God be not only named and officially welcomed, but given a place of precedence and constantly referred to in the U.N., we shall have to bear that accusation with what equanimity we can achieve. But we have a right to expect that those who don't feel as we do about God and Christ and the Christian religion, should at least recognize the fact that we are acting in accordance with conscience. Instead of doing so they accuse us of inhumanity. The fact is that we who look to a spiritual and religious unity have a richer and deeper humanitarianism than those whose ambition would be satisfied with a diplomatic and parliamentary unity.

One of our essential doctrines is that of the Mystical Body—all mankind One in Jesus Christ the Incarnate God.

As a matter of historical fact we have a tradition of world unity. Many centuries ago, in the much maligned—maligned because misunderstood—medieval times, our Church had achieved a united Christendom, not indeed complete and perfect, but more nearly so than any unity that has been known since. England, Ireland, Scotland, Prussia, Bavaria, Italy, France, Spain, the Netherlands, all Scandinavia, indeed before the 10th century the Eastern and Western Worlds, all the countries now shut off from civilization by the Iron Curtains—all were at one. The principle of unity was rejected when the papacy was repudiated. The divisive principle was proclaimed: *Cujus regio ejus religio.* Each kingdom, dukedom, principality was to follow the religion of its ruler. The scriptural principle, "One Lord, One Faith, One Baptism" was forgotten or, if remembered, repudiated. Whether the benefits of discussion outweighed the disadvantages of what was done in the name of freedom may perhaps be a moot question. But the rending of the seamless robe of Christ was, in our view, a calamity. In the face of the world-wide menace of atheism, a return to unity is not only desirable but imperative. "Unite or die," said the American colonists in combat with the imperial power of Britain. Likewise Christendom had better unite or it may perish. Christendom is by definition the dominion of Christ. Can we reconstruct His dominion by leaving Him out?

The indispensability of a United Christendom has been noted again and again from the days when Jesus made His prayer to the Father in the Garden of Olives the night before He died, to those of St. Paul, St. Augustine and all the Fathers of the Church and to the days of the recent and present occupants of the See of Peter. In 1900 Leo XIII in the Encyclical "Jesus Christ Our Redeemer," after quoting St. Paul, "There is no other name under heaven whereby men may be saved than the name of

Jesus," went on to say: "Never to have known Jesus Christ is the greatest of misfortunes. After having known, to reject or forget Him, is such a horrible and mad crime as to be scarcely credible. For He is the origin and source of all good, and just as mankind could not be freed from slavery but by the sacrifice of Christ, so neither can it be preserved but by His power."

The successors of Leo XIII have repeated the same message. To quote only one instance let us choose from the Lenten Message of Pius XII in 1954: "There is no doubt that the words and actions of Christ should penetrate positively everywhere to vivify every one and everything. There is no other solution for humanity but to build the world anew in the spirit of Christ. He alone, in truth, is the Savior of the individual, the family, society as a whole. Let men in high places come to realize the absolute necessity of this, because by ignoring God or denying Him they will build even more precariously than at present."

On March 6, 1955 Archbishop Cushing of Boston said in a public address: "The revolution that is looked for can have only one source and inspiration. The world can be united only by the God Who created it, and only when the human beings upon whom God has bestowed the riches of the world determine to make use of them in accordance with God's laws. An international federation which excludes God from its deliberations and regards religion as a curious psychological phenomenon can never become a principle of unity among men whose deepest longing is for God and whose religious life, persisting in recognizable patterns despite all efforts to crush it, express their instinctive determination to keep close to God even here below."

Chapter 27

World Unity II

THE ARGUMENT in the preceding essay may seem to some readers invalid because it involves the supernatural. We are a curiously illogical race. We declare officially that ours is a Christian civilization, but when we construct an organization to save that civilization we dispense with Christ. In Congress we invoke the name of God but having offered Him that perfunctory obeisance we make no further reference to Him. Debates are held, resolutions passed, laws enacted without so much as a "by your leave" addressed to the Deity. Public officials take oath on the Bible, and from time to time they quote a text as an embellishment in a speech, but they make no pretense of conducting political and diplomatic business in accordance with, shall we say, the Sermon on the Mount. That innocent seeming document is loaded—loaded, as many social reformers have said, with enough dynamite to blow our artificially constructed society to kingdom come. "Search the Scriptures," says the Lord, but we do not search them. We only skim them. "He that readeth let him understand." We read and do not understand. "I am come to cast fire on the earth," says Jesus. But when G. K. Chesterton says "There is fire enough in the Gospels, even when watered down, to set the world ablaze," we say "How fond the fellow is of paradox," and let it go at that.

But to return: when we say that the United Nations Organization can have no success because it bans the name of God, there are those who dismiss the remark as pietistic. They say,

"Let's keep the discussion on the plane of natural reason and avoid recourse to the supernatural." I might at this moment having dropped one digression, pick up another, and develop the thesis that the worst possible dichotomy is the separation of the natural from the supernatural, the alienation of God from His world. "Thy kingdom come," we say, but with the mental reservation, "not here and now."

However, having dutifully repudiated the idea that in the conducting of our worldy affairs we can dispense with the supernatural, I shall make a concession to those who think otherwise and say simply that civilization cannot be served by any deliberative and legislative body which neglects the natural virtues—honesty, sincerity, intellectual and moral consistency. I think it demonstrable that the U.N. has not acted in accord with these indispensable virtues.

The successor to the League of Nations has learned nothing from the collapse of its predecessor. That ill-fated organization was launched with quite as much fanfare as the U.N.; it received an even warmer welcome from the stricken peoples of the world; it drew upon equally generous resources; its champions were no less vocal than those of the United Nations. But the project failed. I say rather it petered out ignominiously. But with that tragic example of futility before their eyes, the founders of the United Nations and its officials to this day have persisted in the same mistakes that ruined the earlier experiment.

Don Luigi Sturzo, an enthusiastic and enlightened advocate of both ventures, says in his *Nationalism and Internationalism*: "Comparing the past with the present, one can see the similarities despite the apparent differences . . . The U.N. has maintained the principle of the League [unanimity] while restricting it to the Big Five. The situations in fact are identical . . . As the four or five [really two, Great Britain and France] powers of the League brought to Geneva their political dualism and their lack of psychological understanding and caused the ruin of

Europe and the world, so today the five, really three [Great Britain, Russia and the United States] have transported to the plane of international organization their political interests and their lack of psychological understanding."

The earlier and the later venture have both committed more than political and psychological blunders. The League was dishonest and so is the U.N. The League pretended to incorporate the 14 Points of Woodrow Wilson, among them, "Open Covenants Openly Arrived At" and "Self Determination for Small Nations." But at Versailles it quickly became evident that the Big Powers claimed for themselves rights and privileges that were denied to the small peoples. The Big Four took over; then the Big Three and finally the Big Two. The principle of "Open Covenants" was even more brazenly violated. There was a joke current in 1918 that the League met in a Hall of Mirrors so that the delegates might see what was happening behind their backs. But mirrors are no deterrent to adepts in the art of diplomatic legerdemain. Behind the back of Woodrow Wilson secret commitments were made as in the days of Bismarck, Disraeli, Metternich, Talleyrand. Was it an old line diplomat who said *"plus ça change, plus c'est la même chose"*? Diplomatic procedure pretends to have reformed but it remains addicted to its inveterate vices.

As in 1918, so today. The head of the London Bureau of *The New York Times* (Feb. 27, 1955) wrote in a gently cynical vein about "Open covenants unopenly arrived at," and he continued: "We must learn all over to reverse our field and run the other way. The salvation of the world was to be in Open Covenants, but that principle is now found inadmissible; we must go back to the old line diplomacy of the Congress of Vienna."

The reason for the abandonment of open diplomacy, the correspondent went on to explain, is that Soviet Russia has always presented itself to its people as "infallible and omniscient" and if its negotiations were conducted in the open, the people of

Russia would learn that they had been deceived. So! Communism deceives the people and we must co-operate in hiding the deception. That would seem to be the reason of the meetings of the Big Four and the Big Three (contemporary version) at Geneva and elsewhere. Too fierce a light beats upon the U.N. Headquarters on the bank of the East River in New York. So, as even the friends of the U.N. confess, it has ceased to be an instrument for the enforcement of peace and has become a "forum for the mobilization of world opinion." By what means non-Communist or anti-Communist opinion is to break its way through the barrier of the Iron Curtain, the U.N. advocates do not explain. But that is a matter of secondary importance, what is paramount is that after ten years the U.N. has abandoned hope of being what it was created to be.

Even when matters of grave importance are introduced in the General Assembly there is no assurance that they will be continued and concluded in the U.N. Members who disapprove of the trend of discussion simply vacate the chamber. In November 1954 Carlos Romulo, former president of the Assembly, wrote: "We are steadily sapping the strength by by-passing it . . . France walks out when the Assembly takes up its disputes with the North Africa Nationalists; Israel and its Arab adversaries pay no attention to U.N. resolutions; India and Pakistan wrangle over conditions for a U.N. decreed plebiscite in Kashmir." Obviously there can be no practical result of discussions in such a forum. There remains only force. Force implies sanctions and the enforcement of sanctions mean war. To enforce peace by means of war is to revert to the oldest method known to imperial powers. "They make a solitude and call it peace," said Tacitus. As Clausewitz has said, "The conqueror is always a lover of peace." He will have peace even if peace be in the midst of a vast wilderness. The U.N. War in Korea (a war under any other name remains a war) should dissuade us from ever again imagining that we can enforce peace upon any spot on the globe by means of arms. Yet without resort to armies, a world organization for the creation and maintenance of peace can be only a debating club.

Besides honesty and sincerity we must have common sense. Without the centripetal force of realism the centrifugal force of idealism will tear the world apart. The world has no doubt suffered much from sordid and brutish realism, but it may be questioned whether realism or a misguided idealism has done the more harm. Enthusiasm is a virtue but enthusiasts are often a menace to peace, justice, right, and perhaps above all to religion.

A still more serious fault—be it intellectual or moral or both—is in the very name of "United Nations." United for what? United in what? Are the United States of America and the United Soviet States of Russia really united? Is there really anything they have in common? Sometimes to the word "nations" the designation is added "peace loving." Can that adjective be applied to us and to Russia in any but an equivocal sense? Are all the excluded nations non-peace-loving? It is not necessary to be specific. One or two samples will do. Ireland was in the League and Ireland's Prime Minister Eamon de Valera was for a term president of the League. Did Ireland cease to be peace-loving between the demise of the league and the birth of the U.N.? What of Italy? She was for a time Fascist. But is a Fascist nation forever after non-peace loving? And Poland? And Finland? And Switzerland? And Spain? We need not multiply instances. The dishonesty in the composition of the U.N. as in its administration is obvious. The first requisite of a court—the U.N. is in part a court—is impartiality.

Finally—for the moral defects of the U.N. are too many to be considered one by one—its supreme fault is in the enormous hiatus between its profession and its action. The second and third paragraphs in the preamble to the Charter of the United Nations read: "To reaffirm faith in fundamental human rights, in the dignity and worth of the human person, in the equal rights of

men and women and of all nations large and small; to establish
conditions under which justice and respect for the obligations
arising from treaties and other sources of international law can
be maintained." That Charter was signed on June 26, 1945.
On June 20, 1949 the United Nations Commission on Human
Rights adopted a "Covenant" outlawing arbitrary arrest, torture,
slavery, forced labor and other such crimes against the dignity
of human beings. But in June, July, August, September 1955
the United States was still humbly beseeching the U.S.S.R.
to release American service men from Communist prisons
where they had been tortured, "brain-washed" and treated
with indignities about which some of the victims said they
could not bring themselves to speak. The point is not that the
Communist regime in Russia, having signed the Charter and
the Covenant, has continued to violate them for ten years. That
fact is notorious. But while we blame Russia for perfidy and
cruelty, we have failed to charge the United Nations with delin-
quency and moral cowardice. In an interview published in *U.S.
News and World Report*, Nov. 26, 1954, Henry Cabot Lodge,
being asked, "Do you mean that if we had it to do over again
Soviet Russia might not have been in the United Nations,"
replied "Absolutely! I do mean that." If Russia would not be
permitted to come in, why is Russia permitted to stay in?

But this chapter has become too long. A full discussion of the
matter in hand would require a book. Suffice it to say by way of
hurrying to a conclusion that no organization which fails to take
the means, natural and supernatural, for success can hope to
contribute to the advancement of civilization.

Chapter 28

Social Justice

THE MOST pathetic fact in the history of civilization is that the race learns very slowly what is for its social and moral good. Man takes an unconscionably long time to get hold of an ethical principle, and a still longer time to apply it in daily life. One would imagine, for example, that slavery would have vanished promptly when the Gospels were once accepted by kings and emperors and people. The master of the other man's life is madly at variance with the Sermon on the Mount. But nations that called themselves Christian did not abolish slavery until 1800 years after Christ.

As of slavery, so in a lesser degree of class distinctions and what St. Paul calls "fables and endless genealogies." Since we are all children of the same father, it is ridiculous that some should call themselves aristocrats, "the best people," as if they had come down body and soul from heaven while the rest of us were common clay. Even if one cannot grasp the noble idea of the brotherhood of man, a little common sense, it would seem, should enable us to laugh at aristocratic pretentions. As Bobby Burns has it:

> You see young birkie, ca'd a lord,
> Wha struts, and stares, and a' that;
> Tho' hundreds worship at his word,
> He's but a coof for a' that;
> For a' that, and a' that,

His ribbon, star, and a' that,
The man of independent mind,
He looks and laughs at a' that.

But even Bobby Burns' proud countrymen are to this day so eager for ribbons and medals and badges and decorations that they accept them from a government that conquered their ancestors.

Certain Christians carry aristocratic distinctions even into church. I wonder what they make of Our Saviour's blunt condemnation of those who "love the first places at feasts and the first chairs in the synagogues" and of His stern condemnation of the Pharisees who thought themselves better than the rest of men. In the Epistle of St. James there is a denunciation of Christians who draw a line of distinction between man and man. "If there shall come into your assembly," says St. James, "a man having a golden ring, in fine apparel, and there shall come in also a poor man in mean attire, and you have respect to him that is clothed with the fine apparel, and shall say to him; 'Sit thou here well'; but say to the poor man; 'Stand thou there or sit under my footstool,' you commit sin" because "you have respect to persons." There's a bombshell for rich pewholders and for the entire breed of snobs who even in church before the altar put up a barrier between themselves and the vulgar horde. The practice of separating nice people from common people persists 1,900 years after St. James and in spite of Jesus Christ.

Take the more important matter of warfare. I suppose we dare not say that any and every imaginable war is sinful and criminal. Self-defense is the first law of nature. But one thing seems certain: we would never go to war unless we were first stirred up to hatred of our fellow man. Yet, according to the Scripture, "He that hateth his brother is a murderer." Wars have continued, and feuds and duels, and race hatred and international animosities, in flat contradiction of the spirit of the Gospel. Indeed we learn slowly.

So it is not to be wondered at if in the matter of social justice the conscience of Christian people has developed very tardily. True, we have got rid of a few of the most obvious instances of man's inhumanity to man. Only in countries that have reverted to paganism is it the custom to condemn multitudes of men and women to penal servitude for no other crime than that of fidelity to conscience. We no longer slaughter captured populations or enslave them. We don't chain captives to the galleys or rivet them to the rock in mines deep in the bowels of the earth. But though the galleys are gone, I doubt if the rowers chained to an oar in a Roman trireme suffered more than the stokers in the hold of a modern steamer, or than the sailors before the mast in the wind-jammers of a generation or two ago. And though mine workers are no longer technically slaves, their lot in life is still desperately hard. I have heard a priest, once a breaker-boy in a Pennsylvania coal mine, tell of his childhood experiences. The story was harrowing. A century after Oliver Twist, we still find it necessary in the Anglo-Saxon world to maintain societies for the Prevention of Cruelty to Children, a scandal, by the way, to the Latins and to the Orientals who cannot understand cruelty to children. Speaking of Oliver Twist, we like to believe that there are no longer schools for teaching children to be pickpockets, but we have boy-bandits in the United States; and indeed an appalling percentage of the prevalent crimes are committed by juveniles and adolescents.

For another social crime, consider the slums in European and American cities—sordid fetid tenements that breed filth, disease, drunkenness, crime, revolt, indecency, obscenity and even degeneracy. They are a stench in the nostrils, literally and figuratively, and a shrieking contradiction of our claim to be a civilized people. With the advance in medical science, hygiene and sanitation, a slum should be impossible, unthinkable. It is less excusable in a modern city than a leper colony amid the rocks and caves and tombs in ancient Palestine. Besides slums, we have huts—huts and hovels in the very shadow of mansions. During the 1929-34 Depression there were on the Hudson River in New York, directly in front of the palatial home of one of the world's wealthiest men, a village of shacks made of bits of waste lumber, fragments of scrap iron, discarded bits of tin, put together with pathetic ingenuity by men, some of them soldiers in the World War, who were not only homeless but destitute and all but starving. The richest city in the world could find no shelter for them. Few passerbys seemed to sense the fact that these pitiable makeshift homes and the still more pitiable occupants of them, were a tragic commentary upon the idea of social justice that prevails in what purports to be the most enlightened community in the world and what is without question the richest. That casual juxtaposition of the millionaire's mansion with hovels fit only for rats but shared by rats and men, must have caused the devils of irony to laugh raucously at the mad inconsistencies of our civilization.

I need not continue the catalogue of these anomalies. Whether the list be long or short we must reach the one conclusion: even here in America we have scarcely commenced to understand the rudiments of social justice. In particular we have been blind and obdurate to the implications of that supreme document of social justice (not to say of the religion that makes our duty to man part of our worship of God), the Gospels of Jesus Christ.

Now there are critics of Christianity—not a few in these days of communism and atheism—who place the blame for the slow development of a sense of social justice at the door of the Church. They might better lay it at the door of human nature. The trouble is not with the Church but with man. The Church teaches but man refuses to learn; the Church cries "Come along" but man lags behind. Any one who questions the fact that the Church, no matter how much a laggard she may seem to the impatient reformer, is always far in advance of the people, might do well to examine his conscience as to whether he keeps pace with the Bible or with the Church in the matter of relationship with his fellow man.

As for the Communists who criticize the entire Christian system as fruitless of social reform, I should imagine that they would have the good grace to be dumb in the face of what organized Communism has done in Russia, in China and in the satellite states. The machine indeed has made progress—terrible progress—amongst the Soviets, especially the war-plane and the battletank, but the dignity of man has been destroyed and his freedom utterly ruined.

Two Popes, Leo XIII in 1891 and Pius XI in 1931 issued encyclicals that have been generally recognized as documents of epoch-making importance, not mere academic statements of doctrine (though they are that) but clarion calls to practice the social justice of the Gospels. In those documents you may find not indeed discussion of intimate details, questions of the valuation of gold and silver, of a federal banking system, of inflation, deflation, reflation, and so on—but fundamental principles which like the roots of a great tree go deep and spread wide. See, for example, how nobly Leo XIII vindicates the dignity of man, the foundation of all social justice:

"No man may with impunity outrage that human dignity which God himself treats with great reverence . . . Nay, more; no man has in this matter power over himself. To consent to any treatment which is calculated to defeat the end and purpose of his being is beyond his right; he cannot give up his soul to servitude; for it is not man's own rights which are here in question, but the rights of God, the most sacred and inviolable of rights."

In consequence man must not be dealt with as if he were an animal or a machine; the work of his hands and the sweat of his brow are not a mere commodity. Pope Pius XI says: "Labor . . . is not a mere chattel, since the human dignity of the working-man must be recognized in it, and consequently it cannot be bought and sold like any piece of merchandise. None the less the demand and supply of labor divides men on the labor market into two classes, as into two camps, and the bargaining between these parties transforms this labor market into an arena where the two armies are engaged in combat."

Popes always speak with moderation, they never give way to hysteria, never play the part of a demogogue, but they do not mince words when they set forth the social evils that are the cause of our present unrest. Take for example such utterances as these from Pius XI: "In our days not alone is wealth accumulated but immense power and despotic economic domination are concentrated in the hands of a few, and those few are frequently not the owners but only the trustees and directors of invested funds, who administer them at their good pleasure.

"This power becomes particularly irresistible when exercised by those who, because they hold and control money, are able also to govern credit and determine its allotment, for that reason supplying, so to speak, the life-blood to the entire economic body, and grasping, as it were, in their hands the very soul of production, so that no one dare breathe against their will."

The pope does not spare his own. He says: "There are even now, some who, while professing the Catholic faith, are well nigh unmindful of that sublime law of justice and charity which binds us not only to give each man his due, but to succor our brethren as Christ, Our Lord Himself; worse still, that there are those who out of greed for gain do not shame to oppress the workingman. Indeed there are some who can abuse religion itself, cloaking their own unjust imposition under its name that they may protect themselves against the clearly just demands of their employees."

It is not my purpose at this time to rehearse the remedies suggested by the popes. I need only say that after showing thus plainly that they visualize the evil, they go on to suggest practical means for reforming the social condition of the world. Some of their principles are so sweeping and, as men say, so "radical" that the world in general is not and for some time to come will not be ready to accept them. To give but one sample. The popes, with the theologians, hold that private wealth is a public trust, and that no man absolutely owns what he happens to possess. Leo says: "The chief and most excellent rule for the right use of money is one which the heathen philosophers hinted at, but which the Church has traced out clearly. It is one thing to have a right to the possession of money, and another to have a right to use money as one wills . . . If the question be asked, How must one's possessions be used? the Church replies without hesitation in the words of St. Thomas Aquinas: 'Man should not consider his material possessions as his own, but as common to all.'"

Call that Communism if you will. It is a noble kind of Communism, infinitely remote from the narrow twisted ill-natured hateful thing rampant in our day and calling itself Communism.

In recent years the sins against social justice have not all been committed by capitalists. It is now notorious that labor unions, grown huge, rich and powerful, ruthless, have to a degree turned the tables upon those who had been oppressors of the poor. Labor leaders have become quite as tyrannical as the capitalists of years ago, and the people at large have come to condone the sins and crimes of Labor. We have lived to see an anomaly: the employer oppressed by the employee, cruelty and injustice suffered by the class which only yesterday ceased, perforce, to be cruel and unjust. Stranger still, yet perhaps not really strange in a world that forever runs from one extreme to another, professional Labor which has quite generally come to violate justice and right, does so in the name of philanthropy, humanity and religion.

It is indeed true that we learn social justice, in particular the social justice of the Gospels, slowly, if at all.

Chapter 29

Christianity, Challenge Or Compromise?

SOMEHOW the impression has come to prevail, especially in recent times, that Christianity is a complacent sort of religion, of an almost effeminate softness, pliant, non-resistant, a religion which accommodates itself readily to all varieties of belief and practice, and is much more apt for compromise than for conflict.

It cannot be denied that there are ostensible reasons for this view of our Faith. We are accustomed to salute our Savior as "Dear Jesus," "Sweet Jesus," we sing to Him, "Gentle Jesus, meek and mild." We refer to Him as the "Humble Nazarene," "The Prince of Peace," "The Good Shepherd"; we call ourselves His flock, that is to say His sheep and reversing the metaphor, we salute Him as the "Lamb of God," who was "led to the slaughter, not opening His mouth." We preach His gospel of non-resistance, using for text that difficult counsel, "If one strike thee on the right cheek, turn to him the other also." Indeed it is possible that we over-emphasize the element of gentleness and sweetness in Christianity.

It is not strange therefore that certain aggressive critics have assailed the religion of Jesus as non-virile and bloodless. Nietzsche, for example, constantly jibes at us as "sheep." Even friendly observers have been scandalized at what seems to them the enervating, devitalizing, one might almost say fatalistic, Buddhistic element in the Gospel, or at least in that part of the Gospel which we call the Sermon on the Mount. Years ago Francis G. Peabody, then professor of Christian Morals at Harvard, in the course of a famous series of lectures at Yale, quoted many such criticisms, among them one from a certain F. H. Bradley who wrote in the *International Journal of Ethics*: "We have lived a long time now the professors of a creed which no one can consistently practice and which if practised would be as immoral as it is unreal."

But the Christian religion is not all milk and honey, not all "hearts and flowers," and most decidedly not a sleeping potion or a drug. I remember that when some time ago in a bit of writing, I praised William Lyon Phelps of Yale as a good Christian, some devout woman sent me the report of a speech in which the professor had said, "Jesus was a trouble-maker, a challenging and a provocative nuisance," and demanded to know how the doctor could be a good Christian and say that. For answer I referred the lady to the Gospels and asked her to observe that Jesus was *exactly that* in the eyes of a world that desired no rousing from its moral and spiritual apathy. There are terrible texts in that sweet Gospel: "Do not think that I came to send peace upon earth. I came not to send peace, but the sword . . ." "I am come to cast fire on the earth." "If the world hate you, know ye that it hath hated Me before you." "Blessed are you when they shall revile you, and persecute you, and speak all that is evil against you." "Yes, the hour cometh, that whosoever killeth you, will think that he doth a service to God." The real Gospel is not pap. It is red meat. The Lamb of God was also the Lion of the Tribe of Juda.

In one chapter of Sir John Seeley's *Ecce Homo*—a chapter significantly entitled "Christ's Winnowing Fan"—he says: "To listen to Christ was no amusement for an idle hour. His preaching formed no convenient resort for lightminded people . . . His words spread around Him a perpetual ferment, an everseething effervescence." As it was in His day, so should it be in ours. The Gospel is not really a soporific but a stimulant. Persons who sleep in their pews during the sermon or, as is more likely nowadays, doze in an armchair at home while a radio or T.V. sermon floats softly into their ears like a lullaby, must not imagine that they are undergoing a religious experience. Good preaching sounds reveille, not taps.

It is part of our Catholic faith that Christ is not only true God but true Man, not a languishing, characterless neutral, neither-God-nor-man. There are sentimental *dilettanti* who tell us how much they love *Il poverello*, St. Francis of Assisi. If St. Francis could appear to them as he really was they would think him a fanatic or a mad man, as the more fastidious Assisians did. Likewise, there are, it is to be feared, multitudes of "pious" people who would not recognize Christ Himself if He suddenly stood before them. They have in their mind's eye a Botticelli if not a Bouguereau Christ, perhaps a pre-Raphaelite Christ, pale and wan and languishing. They don't care for the Michelangelo Christ of The Last Judgment. But Michelangelo makes Him what He was—a man.

But to return to the question of Christ as a "trouble-maker, a challenge and provocative nuisance." It is the simple truth that no one ever irritated more people and more different kinds of people than He. There is a saying, familiar to students of ancient Christian controversy, *Athanasius contra mundum*. Even more justly we say *Christus contra mundum*: Christ alone against the whole world. And the world that opposed Him was a gigantic power. He was caught between the upper and the nether millstone, the Romans and the Jews, and between them He knew He would be ground to powder.

Now what does a weak man do when he finds himself all alone against the powers that be? He compromises, he keeps silent; he bides his time; he finds excuses for not beginning his work; he fills his mouth with maxims about prudence; he soothes his soul by reflections on the hopelessness of the situation; he eases his conscience with the consideration that God cannot command impossible things, that no man need court certain death.

But Christ was no weakling. He could not compromise. He had work to do and He would do it. He had something to say, and He would say it. He would not desist till His voice was smothered in His own Blood. He beheld His people misguided by a set of narrow, fanatical, casuistical bigots, and He would warn the people and scourge the bigots. He saw a nation being led into error by a jabbering crowd of blind theological guides. He saw an organization of hypocrites devouring the houses of widows, praying long prayers with bogus piety. In His eyes that hypocrisy and fraud cried to heaven for punishment. He saw the money-grabbers making the house of prayer a den of thieves, and He would put them to rout single-handed; He saw the lordly Pharisees wearing their phylacteries broad upon their foreheads, receiving salaams and salutations in the market-place, and He would bring down their pride by telling them that they were worse than the publicans and the harlots. They considered themselves the salt of the earth, the elect among mankind, the cream of the people of God, and He would tell them to their teeth, that they were whited sepulchers full of dead men's bones and all rottenness. He saw the conscience of the people misdirected by a group of charlatans, and He would tear off the veil and expose the impostors before the eyes of the people who had almost worshipped them. They thought they had the keys of the kingdom of heaven, that when they opened no man could shut and when they shut no man could open. But He told them that they were closing the kingdom of heaven against men and that they would never themselves enter in. And not to attempt to mention each one of the articles of the stinging indictment of Christ against the Pharisees, He called them "Blind guides, fools and blind, children of hell, serpents, a generation of vipers full of rapine and uncleanness, murderers of the prophets, upon whose hands was the blood of every messenger of God from Abel to Zacharias," and He predicted that they should not escape the "judgment of hell."

Christ was a prophet in the old tradition. Yes, more than a prophet. Sometimes I like to indulge the imagination as to what might have happened if Pontius Pilate had had a stiffer backbone. He knew that Jesus had done nothing worthy of death under the Roman law, but he could not deny the accusations of the Pharisees, "This man stirreth up the people." Suppose Pilate had said to Jesus what a certain administrator whom I used to know said to one who quite legitimately brought him a tale of trouble, "Go home, Sir, and do not disturb my peace of mind." It would doubtless have been phrased differently: "Go home, Galilean, to your native hills. Till your field, or mend your nets, or busy yourself in your carpenter's shop. Cease preaching—at least in this our province of Judaea. Keep away from the streets of Jerusalem. With these thousands who follow after you and thousands of others who oppose you there is bound to be conflict. Let the tumult die down and see that thou stir it not up again."

But in fact Jesus had forestalled this imaginary speech of Pilate's. He had said, "For this was I born and for this I am come into the world that I should give testimony to the Truth." One of His apostles, Paul, was to say later, "Woe is me if I preach not the Gospel." Jesus would no more have gone back to the carpenter's shop and kept His peace than Paul would have gone back to his tent-making. "What though there were turmoil wherever He went? He had observed that fact. He deplored it, but it could not compel Him to subside. Also He foresaw the tragic outcome. With prophetic vision He also dipped into the future and saw that continents would be immersed in a bloody baptism for centuries as a result of His teaching. Jesus knew that there was to be no peace between the Church and the world, the Gospel and pagan philosophy.

Yet he did not waver. He disdained compromise. He went on relentlessly to the inevitable end. Be it remembered furthermore that Christ had no position, no throne, no army, no bodyguard. He enjoyed no immunity from personal danger. Yet He hurled

His thunderbolts into the face of sacrosanct individuals and divine-right potentates, backed by an army and a government that was the mightiest machine of coercion that had ever been organized.

Now the world, *as the world,* has not changed. Hypocrites and charlatans and whited sepulchers still hold high office. A true evangelist cannot write, nor a true apostle speak without irritating them. Christ could not do it, and the disciple is not more skillful than his Master. Jesus Himself said to the Jews, "You killed all the prophets from Abel to Zacharias." After the prophets, all the apostles were killed, all save one and if he was not killed, it was not due to any particular kindness on the part of his enemies—they threw him into a vat of boiling oil! The thirteenth apostle, St. Paul, declared plainly enough, "If I were the friend of men I should not be the servant of God." So he too suffered the inevitable fate of those who tell the truth.

It is necessary I think to remind ourselves of these familiar facts—familiar though forgotten—in our soft times when numbers of timorous Christians demand that their clergymen preach an inoffensive gospel. There is no inoffensive gospel. If the Gospel were lived as it is, unqualified, unadapted, unexpurgated, it would turn civilization upside down as it did once before.

I shall not close without admitting that the element of vigor does not comprise the entire character of Christ, or of Christianity. Our religion I have said, is not all roses and lilies. But neither is it all blood and iron. Paradoxically it is both gentle and stern, sweet and severe. Just as a man can be at once kind and strong, just as Jesus was both Lion and Lamb, true religion can be and is a sweet consolation and a fiery stimulus. To forget or to minimize either of these characteristics is to have an incomplete comprehension of Christianity.

Chapter 30

Escape from Life

MY CONCERN in this essay is not with the miseries and the wretchedness of life, but with the possibility of escape from those miseries and that wretchedness. What with wars, rumors of wars, fears and threats of wars; industrial strife forever smoldering and often bursting forth in riot and sometimes in revolution—industrial revolution more savage than political revolution; what with cruelty and tyranny that in ancient and medieval times used to be intermittent and emotional but that in our day is deliberately inflicted with a persistence and an efficiency hitherto unknown; tyranny more prolonged, systematic, comprehensive than that of Herod or Nero or Peter the Great; purges, pogroms, persecutions; what with repudiation of the plighted word of nations; a policy of deceit and perjury in place of honorable diplomatic intercourse; what with the increasing triumph of bullies, alias "dictators," and the consequent complete rout of statesmanship; what with the swift growth of domestic immorality, especially as it regards sex-relations; what with the debasement of art and music—the substitution of jungle rhythms in place of melody and harmony, the insane vogue of jitterbug dancing and of obscene theatrical entertainment; what with literature more brazen than at any time since the licentious days of Charles II; and, worst of all, what with the apprehension, which can be sensed in the very atmosphere, that the end is not yet, but that worse things are to come; under these conditions, I say, we have arrived at the time when any sort of escape might seem justified.

The basest, stupidest, most ordinary means of attempted escape is drink. I call it base, even though the philosophical poet Omar Khayyam justifies the use of the grape as a narcotic. He says:

> Yesterday this day's madness did prepare,
> Tomorrow's silence, triumph or despair.
> Drink for you know not whence you came nor why,
> Drink for you know not why you go or where.

And again:

> Fill the cup that clears
> Today of past regrets and future fears.

The tentmaker has something of a reputation as a philosopher, but in this case his logic is that of the opium eater or of the Oriental beggar who whines "An alms, for the love of Allah"— an alms, an alms he should say, for the love of hashish. But drink or drug, the method of escape is ineffective. Hamlet considers the idea that "by a sleep . . . we end the heartache and the thousand natural shocks that flesh is heir to," but he sees the objection "To sleep, perchance to dream, Aye there's the rub, For in that sleep of death what dreams may come!"

When the sleep is not the sleep of death but of drink or of drugs, a worse fate is in store for the escapist. To sleep, to dream, *to wake,* aye there's the rub, to wake again to the heartache and the thousand shocks that one had hoped to escape. In Greek mythology there was a river Lethe in which the bather could find oblivion. Unfortunately Lethe was a river in Hades. When the bather emerged from the waters he found himself still in hell, a hell that seemed worse because he had to come back to it. Shrewd myth-makers those ancient Greeks! There are methods of attempted escape which only accentuate one's miseries.

There was always an element of realism in the Greek philosophy. But further east in India is the land beyond all others fecund with philosophies that run to the mystical—pseudo-mystical, rather than to the rational. Chief of these was, and is, Buddhism. Buddha held the view that existence and even more the will or desire to exist was an unmitigated evil; that the only wisdom is to outwit, as it were, whatever Malevolent Power gave life to man and implanted in his breast a love of life. There is, said Buddha, a way out of life, not only this life but any and all life; the way is long and arduous involving many reincarnations, births and rebirths, deaths and returns from death, but if one will but follow a rigorous formula, he can eventually find Nirvana—Oblivion. Buddha, therefore, is represented as sitting on his haunches, legs crossed, eyes shut in a trance. He has eyes but sees not, ears but hears not; he is "serene, indifferent to fate," altogether unaware of the teeming life of the Orient all about him, unconcerned about the miseries of men, even though beneath him and before him, in India and China, there is perhaps more wretchedness than anywhere else in the world. Perhaps it is for that reason that his eyes are forever closed: he must maintain his unnatural serenity; he *must not* see. Flood and famine and plague happen before his very face; they take their terrible toil—millions of human lives—but Buddha remains blissfully, or shall we say stupidly and callously unaware that calamity has befallen his devotees. War, bloodshed, slaughter occur so close to him that the blood of his victims spatters his statue and drenches his shrine; cries of mourning and lamentation and woe ascend to his ears but he sees not, hears not, minds not. He sits and sleeps the sleep of stupefaction. It is his philosophy, his idea of the way to bliss, to be blind and deaf and dumb and unconcerned.

Such is the typical Oriental technique of escape. There have been hundreds of millions who have adopted that heartless soulless philosophy as a way of life, as a religion.

The present rulers of Russia have taken up the Marxian slogan as the keynote of atheistic propaganda, "Religion is the opium of the people." A great portion of the territory of Russia is in Asia, and the Russians are largely and characteristically Asiatic. The religion of many of them did work like an opiate. Whether no religion at all is better than a religion that stupefies, benumbs, produces inertia, lethargy, inculcates indifference to poverty, sickness, death, and all other causes of grief; a religion that meets all human problems by shutting the eyes, or turning the back— whether no religion at all is better than such an inhuman or subhuman religion, I think, may be debated. If the Communists have Buddhism in mind and other religions of the Far East in which the Buddhist influence is notable, religions that in effect produce paralysis of the mind and the heart, of intelligence and emotion, I think we might agree, in that one instance, with the Communists. If a people is cursed with that kind of religion they might perhaps better clean it all away and start anew, as they will start soon again, with a religion that will wake them up and make them live.

G. K. Chesterton has remarked with his customary acumen that whereas the images of Buddha are all seated and asleep, the images of our saints stand erect with their eyes wide open. And many a Catholic commentator has made a point of the fact that St. Stephen the first martyr standing erect in the midst of the mob until he was felled by the stones they hurled at him, lifting up his eyes to heaven said, "I see . . . the Son of man *standing* on the right hand of God." Our God is no sitting God, blind and deaf, inert, stupefied, paralyzed. As Jesus said Himself, "He is not the God of the dead but of the living." If any man in India or China or Russia, or, for that matter, in this western world, has a sleeping God or a sleeping religion, he might for a moment at least be better off with no God and no religion. What we want is not an escapist God or an escapist religion, but a God and a religion that are wide awake, alive to the condition of humankind upon this globe, and not only alive and awake but eager and able to do something to make the world better and man happier even here below.

And that, I think, is what the popes have in mind when they recommend Catholic Action. Not passivity, not lethargy, not mental and spiritual stupefaction, not a run-away-from-the-facts religion, but a stand-up-face-the-facts-and-do-something-about-it religion. Ours is indeed an Oriental religion, partly. It came out of the east, the near east; there is in it a degree of serenity, a considerable element of peace and quiet, but it is the peace and quiet and confidence of a soldier on the battlefield, not of a drug addict asleep on a bunk in an opium "joint" while a conflagration rages all around him. Our religion is a stimulant, not a narcotic. A text often heard in our pulpits runs, "The life of man upon earth is a warfare." The ancient patriarch Job didn't look the part of a warrior, stricken on his dunghill, covered with sores and teased with the reproaches of his merciless friends. But the big fact in our religion is that a naked man on a dunghill, hideous with ulcers and overwhelmed with the contumely of curious spectators of his miseries, such a man may none the less be fighting a good fight. Indeed ours is a fighting religion, though the weapons of our warfare are not carnal, but spiritual. The very fact that we are and have been persecuted and proscribed in one country and another, generation after generation, is evidence of the fact that even our enemies see in us a living force. We don't lift a hand or fire a shot; but we are a danger to dictators and tyrants. Instinctively they recognize the fact and in consequence they threaten us with extinction. According to an old adage, "Imitation is the sincerest flattery." But opposition is even more of a compliment than imitation. We could escape opposition if we would, but we have no desire to escape. We are not an escapist religion.

There is in the modern world another system which has, I think, an affinity with Buddhism. It holds that the evils of the world can be best dealt with by a refusal to acknowledge their existence. Poverty, sickness, warfare, bloodshed, vice, crime, all manner of misfortunes are produced, so it holds, by thinking. They have no real existence. They are illusions created like the poet's fancies out of "airy nothing." They would vanish like the mists of the morning if we would but declare that they do not exist. Humanity produces its own calamities by thinking of them. The cure would be the same as the cause—thinking. We think ourselves into predicaments; we should think ourselves out of predicaments.

Evidently this is not precisely Buddhism. It is optimistic, not pessimistic. One does not close the eyes to evil, one closes the mind. Nirvana, oblivion, is not the goal, though it must be confessed that the literature of the subject seems to say that the end of human life is absorption in the Divine. Yes, there are surface differences, but unless my sense of logic is at fault, there is a spiritual relationship between Orientalism and this philosophico-religious faith. To deny the existence of sin and sorrow, of battles and blood and wounds, of disease and death, in the very face of manifest fact does at least make this a religion of escape. Of course, like other escapist theories and systems, it does not really produce escape. It would be exceedingly hazardous tactics to forego the practice of medicine when small pox or yellow fever or the "flu" threatens. Just about as hazardous as for an army drawn up in battle array to lay down its arms on the theory that the army on the other side of "No-man's land" doesn't really exist; that its movements are a mirage, its shot and shell and gas, its bombs dropped from airplanes, all a trick of the imagination. The army that laid down its arms on such a theory might indeed escape—if by escape you mean annihilation.

There remains yet another philosophy that had a great vogue at about the time of the origin of the Christian religion. It was called Stoicism. It prevailed in Greece and Rome especially amongst the intellectuals who thought themselves too enlightened to hold the ancient and primitive mythologies.

The Stoic cultivated philosophic calm, polite contempt for the vulgar horde of mankind, and a quietly scornful attitude towards fate. His creed may be said to be comprised in two phrases *"Non turbari,"* and *"nil admirari"*: be not disturbed, be not surprised at anything. The perfect Stoic was the geometer who drew mathematical figures on the sand of the beach as Alexander the Great swept on his all-conquering march into the neighboring city. World conquest meant nothing to the Stoic, nor bloodshed, loot, rape, flame and sword; not for that matter the slaughter of the soldiers who had manned the walls to protect their own, nor the death of helpless women and innocent children along with the soldiers. To the Stoic nothing matters, nothing except self-possession, calm, poise, mental equilibrium. All emotion, all enthusiasm is vulgar, unworthy of a philosopher. If there be a third word in the Stoic creed it is the Greek word *apatheia,* that is to say "passionlessness." All passions are tabu to the Stoic, good passions or bad, love, hate, fear, hope, even the passion for right and justice, even an over-earnest concern about truth and honor. If there were one maxim more than all others abhorrent to the Stoics in Rome or at Athens who first heard strange uncouth bearded Jews from Palestine preaching the Gospel, it was "Thou shalt love the Lord thy God with thy whole heart, and with thy whole soul, and with thy whole mind, and with thy whole strength." The Stoic did nothing with all his mind and heart and soul and strength. Had he done so he would have gone out of himself, and the prime tenet of his philosophy was that he should remain within himself. When he heard Paul of Tarsus on the Areopagus, the worst thing he could think to say was, "Paul, thou art beside thyself," as though Paul had leaped out of his own skin. The Stoic stayed inside his own skin, given over entirely to the contemplation of his own mind. The great emperor Marcus Aurelius, perhaps the most famous of all the Stoics, both as a philosopher and as a ruler, said that he took refuge from the affairs of State by retiring into his own mind.

John Cowper Powys said: "Aurelius is one of the weariest, saddest, most heartbroken Stoics who ever lived. He is a philosopher for the unhappy; for he himself was unspeakably unhappy. Underneath all his labors and honors and triumphs there lies *an ice-cooled pool of despair."*

Over against all these strangely abnormal and inhuman philosophies of escape, there stands the religion of Jesus Christ, a marvelous synthesis of the real and the ideal. The Gospel contains many a hard saying, much sadness, and one supreme tragedy, to say nothing of the many lesser tragedies. But it is none the less a happy and triumphant document. So Christianity admits the pathetic and the tragic elements in human life, but it is none the less a joyous, even a jubliant, optimistic, triumphant faith. We aim to conquer sin and vice and crime not by shutting the eyes to them, still less by turning tail and running away, but by meeting them full face on, as Jesus met His enemies in the garden of Gethsemani, in the streets of Jerusalem, in the courts of Pilate and Herod. Had He been an escapist He would have remained hidden away in the folds of the hills about Nazareth. But the Gospel says, "He steadfastly set His face to go to Jerusalem." He went, He looked the Pharisees in the eye; He opened His mouth and poured out upon them a torrent of invective. He did not pretend not to see their sins; He was not blind to grievances of the poor people whom they afflicted. He faced sinners, not with some fine-spun philosophy about their sin being an illusion; not with some recondite psychological theory about no man's being really responsible for his deeds. To lie about an evil, to dissemble, to invent fantastic theories, to shut the eyes and the ears and to be mute, to harden the heart and paralyze the soul into insensitiveness, these are not the methods of combatting sin. No, nor the retiring into an ice-cold pool of passionlessness in one's own heart. Nor the seeking of peace, interior peace, at any cost. "Do not think that I came to send peace upon earth: I came not to send peace, but the sword." The sword of the spirit, of course, not the sword reeking with blood. The moral sword, the sword of truth and justice; for our religion, serene and sweet and lovable though it be, is a fighter's religion. We look for no Nirvana here or hereafter, no absorption in the Divine or in Oblivion. We look for life in this world and beyond—life abundant, vigorous, pulsating, personal, conscious, the supreme life of a divine ecstasy. We plan to achieve that life in whatever degree possible here on earth, but perfectly in the kingdom of heaven. We aim not to escape life, but to "lay hold on eternal life, whereunto [we] are called." And we shall lay hold on that life when we have taken the kingdom by storm. That kind of religion is the remotest possible antithesis to Buddhism, Stoicism, or Occidental forms of escapism.

Chapter 31

Freedom from the Mass Mind

AMERICANS in general believe in Democracy. We are dedicated to it. Some of us are so devoted to Democracy that we are not content to possess it ourselves but are all afire to communicate it to the rest of the world as if it were a gospel or a Divine Revelation. So impetuous is our zeal that we don't stop to ask the rest of the world if it wants Democracy. "My house," said the jocular host, "is Liberty Hall: under this roof you do what you please: if you don't, we make you." Certain extravagant devotees of Democracy think that all the world must value what we value and live as we live or be compelled to do so.

We would die for Democracy, but don't ask us to define Democracy. Does it mean, in accordance with the old Latin maxim, *Vox populi, Vox Dei,* "The voice of the people is the voice of God"? Does it mean not only that officials are elected but that justice is determined by majority vote? Does it mean that when the people have solemnly declared their judgment, their judgment is infallible? Are questions of right or wrong, true or false, to be decided by vote? Granted that the question of war or peace may be decided by majority vote—majority of the people or majority of the representatives of the people—does that vote carry with it a guarantee that the war is a just war or the peace a righteous peace?

Hundreds of critical and caustic questions like these are flung at us by those who prefer a dictatorial government. They assail what they call "the democratic principle" of determining matters

196

of infinite importance by the ridiculous process of counting noses. If that be the democratic principle it is right to ridicule and rail at it.

I would not go out on a limb with a definition of Democracy. What concerns me here and now is not Democracy in the political sense, but the principle sometimes carried over from the political sphere into the moral world, the principle that if a sufficient number of people follow a course of conduct, that course of conduct must be right and good and true. Whatever be the correct definition of Democracy, that definition is dismally and fatally wrong. Numbers do not make truth. When the first Christians came into the Western World from Palestine they were not one-tenth of one percent of the population even of the Mediterranean area; and, if you set them over against the vaster populations beyond the border of the Empire of the Caesars, they were numerically so insignificant that the Romans and the Persians and the Indians and the Chinese might have considered them not worth counting at all. And yet as the medieval *Chanson de Roland* says, "The heathen are wrong" and the Christians, be they few or be they many, are right. Before the end of the second century the Christian orator Tertullian declared: "We are but of yesterday, yet we fill your cities, islands, forts, towns, councils, camps . . . the palace, the senate, the forum; we have left you only the temples of your gods." It would be dangerous, however, to use that argument in proof of the Christian religion. Later on, Mohammedanism spread as rapidly; and in our own day we have seen in Russia, atheism supplanting religion with incredibly popular acquiescence. It would be a crazy logic that would attempt to prove that Christianity was true in Russia under the Czar, false under Stalin, and true again when Stalin and his associated murderers have gone to their reckoning. Yet that would seem to be the conclusion if the maxim that what the majority decides or what the majority accepts is right.

But that logic and that curious conclusion have a certain vogue here and now in the social and moral world. There are those who justify divorce and remarriage on the ground that "times have changed." The Gospel says that remarriage after divorce is sinful. The people of America three hundred years ago believed that Gospel. But now if the majority of the people have ceased to believe in the Gospels, does that invalidate the teaching of the Son of God on marriage and divorce? Incredible though it may seem I have heard a Protestant clergyman say that the Holy Eucharist was indeed the Real Presence of Christ in the thirteenth century but is no longer His Body and Blood because the greater part of the world has ceased to believe in it.

In the early centuries there was a heresy, Arianism, which denied that Jesus was the Son of God. Various emperors after Constantine favored the heretics and persecuted the Catholics with such violence and such success that as one historian said epigrammatically, "The world awoke to find itself Arian"; and Saint Athanasius, defender of orthodoxy, was "alone against the world." But would any one say that Christ was God while Constantine reigned and ceased to be God under Constantius, or that Christanity was true until Julian the Apostate came to the throne but that thereupon paganism became true again?

Does truth follow the vicissitudes of kingdoms and empires? Did Christ go out and Wotan come in with Hitler? Does religion become "opium" because Lenin and Stalin say so? Does truth dawn and die with the day, ebb and flow with the tide? Are truth and right and justice and virtue subject to the whim of a ruler? "Justice is what the State says it is," according to Thomas Hobbes, an English philosopher two hundred and fifty years before Nazis, Fascists and Communists discovered the idea. But is it? Or is justice as fixed as the stars above a revolving world? Is truth also what the State says it is, or has truth an independent existence, changeless in spite of the everchanging whims of men?

The Declaration of Independence speaks of "unalienable rights." Is that a piece of oratory? Or is it a philosophical and theological truth that the fundamental rights of men remain whether or not kings, empires, parliaments, congresses acknowledge them?

To come to the more particular point I would make. If we deny the right of rulers of men to create or to annihilate right and justice and truth and virtue, shall we concede that right to the people? If a whole people or a majority of the people approves the denial of fundamental rights to a certain race of men, let us say in some places Negroes and in other places Jews, do Negroes and Jews thereby justly forfeit unalienable rights? If a tyrant— man or State—denies the right of Protestant pastors or Catholic priests to preach the Gospel, does the command of Christ, "Go teach," "Go preach," cease upon the moment? "We must obey God rather than man," says St. Peter. Have times changed so that now we must obey men and disobey God?

I use examples from the world of politics only as analogies, but my primary concern is with the moral world. When people speak of "immorality" they usually have in mind indecency, obscenity, or some other violation of holy purity. But is there not a deeper immorality—that which considers moral principle elastic, evanescent, fickle as the whims of man, or of woman. *La donna è mobile,* says the operatic aria, *qual' plum' al vento:* "Woman is fickle as a feather in the wind." Justice is pictured as a woman, and so is Truth. Are Justice and Truth blown hither and thither with every breeze?

The deepest and most dangerous immorality of all is the immorality of those who think that what was true yesterday may be false today or tomorrow; that what was vicious in our grandparents' day is virtuous now; and that a change in ethical principles must follow a change in the mind of the majority of the people.

The same phenomenon appears in the world of business and of the professions. I know many business men, lawyers, physicians who lament the trend to the unethical in the special worlds in which they operate. They tell me that the tide is running against them, that too many of their rivals have reduced business ethics and professional ethics to three principles: "Everybody's doing it": "If I don't do it some one else will"; and "You can't do business nowadays on old-fashioned principles." Especially in metropolitan cities they say the ethical degeneration is obvious. They blame this set of persons or that, but they all seem agreed that decline if not actual decay is upon us. "It is easy enough," they add, "for you preachers to tell us to stand firm, to hew to the line and all that. But we have families to support, homes to maintain, food and clothing to buy. To do business on the morals of a past generation is as impossible as to do business with the methods of the past generation. We must do what the others do or be sunk. We cannot forever buck the stream. They call us fools, fossils, reactionaries if we don't swing in with the multitude."

No priest or preacher can fail to be aware of that objection to traditional business and professional morals. But no moralist, unless he abdicate his position and turn renegade to his vocation, can acquiesce or temporize. Right is right if nobody does it. Wrong is wrong if everybody does it. What the business man needs and what the professional man needs is a new declaration of independence. A century and a half ago here in America our forefathers declared for political independence. It may be that the day has come to declare for moral independence. They declared in 1776 independence from the tyranny of a king; today it may be advisable to declare independence from the majority. As any student of history knows full well, it is easier to defy a Nero or a Caligula or an Ivan or a Hitler or a Stalin than to defy the crowd. Louis XVI was a mild-mannered tyrant, but the mob that came into power when he had been guillotined was the wildest, craziest, most bloodthirsty that the world had known, though they carried banners with the democratic slogan, "Liberty, Equality, Fraternity."

To go further back and higher up, Jesus might have been

spared by Herod—Herod didn't care; or by Pilate—Pilate wanted to be just; but what sealed the doom of our Savior was that mad mob in the streets of Jerusalem. You may ask justice from a tyrannical king. He may listen. But if you speak of justice to a raging mob you only infuriate them the more. Government of the people is a boon and a blessing when the people are sane and just, but when the people become a mob, they are more cruel than Nero or Caligula or Peter the Great.

There remains one other tyranny, social tyranny, which generally slides into moral tyranny. In the world of entertainment, public and private, the world of the theatre, of the dance, of eating and drinking—especially drinking—it is said to be no longer possible to follow one's own will and way, to plan one's own life. If a woman refuses to follow the styles in dress, even though the styles be indecent and perhaps in her case absurd, she must go to no end of inconveniences and expense, and be ready for ridicule.

So also in the world of hospitality. If the lady of the house will not do what others do, if she refuses to conduct a kind of open bar in her home in the presence of her children, a bar at which all visitors may drink, and many will drink to excess, she is considered fanatical. If she makes even a mild protest against her adolescent daughter's late hours, the frequentation of night clubs and indiscriminate companionship, she is denounced by her own flesh and blood as cruel. If she declines to go out night after night, or a dozen times a month to play cards, and to drink strong drink, she acquires the reputation of being unsocial or anti-social. If—now I speak of conditions in oversized metropolitan cities like this one of New York—a mother suggests, however patiently and adroitly, that her boys and girls approaching manhood and womanhood should as a rule avoid places of public entertainment and make their own fun with their own friends in their own home, it will be well if the young people do not exchange significant glances with one another and perhaps make gestures behind her back to indicate that they think her "a hopeless poor dear."

Their argument against all such reasonable suggestions is that "nobody entertains at home; the sing-fest around the piano is 'old hat.' It is not done, mother: it simply isn't done! If we go in for that sort of entertainment we shall have no friends."

A petty tyranny indeed, this last one, but very real, especially to the young. What they need is still another declaration of independence; a resolution to live life sanely and reasonably, to entertain themselves with a supreme disregard of the indecencies, the shamelessness, the bawdiness, the vulgarity, and the banality of the night-club world.

Do boys and girls follow the habits and customs of the world that envelops them? Do they accept perhaps at first with a mild disgust but later without protest the prevalent form and manner of relationship between the sexes? If the majority follows a certain pattern in that matter, must everybody submit to being made over according to the pattern? Must all permit themselves to be regimented and standardized, even though regimentation and standardization mean the surrender of their ideals, their personality, their spiritual independence? To put it in a phrase, are they afraid to call their souls their own?

I fear that if we, or the young folk themselves, answer these questions frankly, we shall have to confess that like their fathers and mothers—fathers in the business and professional world, mothers in the social world—they are victims of the mass mind. They do what they don't wish to do because all the world is doing it.

It is time that we declared our independence of the tyranny of the majority. There are not "Four Freedoms" only. There are Five, and the Fifth is more important than some of the others— Freedom from mass-thinking.

Chapter 32

What Is It All About?

"WHAT's it all about?" is one of those vague indefinite expressions that may mean anything, everything, nothing. At present it happens to be a slang phrase, flung around indiscriminately, sometimes making sense, sometimes nonsense. I have heard an impatient listener at a violin recital say of an incompetent performer, who was floundering around in a Beethoven Sonata, "He doesn't know what it's all about." A spectator at a newsreel depicting a congressman clumsily defending some dubious policy of his party, said in a stage whisper, "He doesn't know what it is all about." Listening to three men of national reputation in a debate I felt that not any of them knew what it was all about. There has appeared in the papers a picture of the great-great-great-grandson of a national hero pulling the string to unveil a statue of his famous ancestor. The little fellow was caught by the camera with such a timid little smile on his face that he seemed about to cry. "The poor child doesn't know what it's all about," said a dear kind lady.

The best known and best liked playwright and comedian of the American stage fifteen or twenty years ago, after dancing and singing and waving a flag all evening would answer a curtain call with a monologue commencing "Life is a funny proposition after all; we're here today and away tomorrow," and meaning not we're on Broadway today and on the road tomorrow, "but we're alive today and dead tomorrow." It was a semi-serious piece, an attempt to puzzle out an answer to the question "What's

It All About?," a sort of Broadway version of Shakespeare's *Seven Ages of Man,* from the infant, "mewling in the nurse's arms," to the "lean and slippered pantaloon" ending "this strange eventful history" of human life in "second childishness and mere oblivion."

"Strange, eventful history," says Shakespeare. The history of man on this planet puzzles, fascinates, baffles dramatists, poets, philosophers, all manner of thinkers, profound and superficial, religious and irreligious. It thrills the idealists, angers the pessimists, and seems to nauseate the cynics. Shakespeare recurs to it again and again both in his comedies and his tragedies. Whether he writes of country buskins like Bottom in "hempen homespun" upon whom the fairies play practical jokes, or of disgruntled amateur philosophers like Hamlet, brooding over "the oppressor's wrong the proud man's contumely" and all the other grievances listed in that familiar soliloquy; whether he treats of a poltroon like Falstaff or of a real soldier "seeking the bubble reputation in the cannon's mouth"; whether of the big blackamoor, honest, stupid, tragic, pathetic Othello, or of some wily devil like Iago or Richard, masquerading in human form, Shakespeare is forever occupied with nothing else but the formidable question, "What's It All About?" Man is born, grows, matures, works, plays, sins, suffers, marries, procreates, rejoices, grieves, sickens, dies. Sometimes he seems like a god upon the earth, or an angel; again, as King David says, "he is compared with senseless beasts and made like to them." Sometimes he seems to be master of his fate, dictator of his destiny, a lord of all creation, but again he is heard complaining like Gloucester in King Lear, "As flies to wanton boys are we to the gods; they kill us for their sport." Beast or angel, man or devil, master or slave, victor or victim, he struts his brief hour upon the stage of life, and passes off; he has his entrance and his exit.

Looking upon human life as spectators at some bewildering play, men ask "What does it mean? What can it mean? What's it all about?" All literature, art, music, poetry, drama and the better sort of fiction—fiction which is not fiction but truth—are really nothing but an attempt to answer these questions. "What's it all about?" asks Shakespeare, and all that he writes—comedies, histories, tragedies—are his answer. Dramatists and philosophers, Sophocles and Socrates, and Seneca and Epictetus, Marcus Aurelius, and ten thousand thinkers in their tradition, aim to interpret human life, that is to say "What's It All About?" Henrik Ibsen, Eugene O'Neill, Thomas Hardy, Schopenhauer, Voltaire, Mark Twain (the later Mark Twain, humorist turned pessimist, the Mark Twain who wrote *The Mysterious Stranger*), Aldous Huxley, Hector Bolitho, author of *Twelve Against the Gods,* Ernst Haeckel, curious combination of charlatan and scientist, author of *The Riddle of the Universe,* Robert G. Ingersoll, probably honest but bombastic and blasphemous—but why prolong the interminable catalogue? All literature in prose and verse, all art and drama and the more ambitious kind of music—Bach, Beethoven, Brahms, Wagner—are all concerned with that seemingly flippant question "What's It All About?" Aristotle said, twenty four hundred years ago, that man is born with an insatiable desire to know. What he wants to know is the meaning of life, and what there is, if anything, after this life, and what is the connection between this life and the other. It's a far cry from Aristotle to George M. Cohan, but the Yankee Doodle Boy who would suddenly swing into the monologue, "Life is a funny proposition after all," was, I suppose, trying to convey to the rather blasé Broadway audiences, something of what Aristotle tried to tell the Greeks on the Areopagus in Athens.

All thinkers great and small since the birth of thought have pondered the questions, "What is Man?" and "What is Life?" Is this the only Life? If there is no other, what can be the purpose of this? If life is, as some one has said, a flash of light between two eternities of darkness, if we emerge out of one black void and disappear into another, "What's it all about?"

St. Paul of course like all profound thinkers—he indeed being the most profound of them all—says that if this were all there is of life Christians should be the "most miserable of men." Undoubtedly the higher our hopes, the deeper our despair. But all other men would be miserable too. No man can be satisfied with this painful thing we call life. With his hopes and desires and anticipations and expectations it would be infernal torture to man to be told that what he suffers, he suffers to no purpose.

Anatole France, who concealed the deep cynicism of a Schopenhauer under the shallow flippancy of a Voltaire, said *"L'Univers est enragé,"* "the universe is mad." The word "enragé" carries, I believe, the connotation of rabid. The French use it of a mad dog. Apparently then, according to Anatole France, the whole world and all men and women in it are suffering like a dog with rabies. We are all mad—not only with ambition, greed, lust, the lust of the flesh or blood lust, but mad especially with hallucinations of grandeur. We think there is something else but there isn't. "Man who elevated himself to the skies," says Ernst Haeckel, "is found to be only a placental mammal, of no more importance in the universe than the microscopic infusoria," the bugs that move blindly in the slime under the murky waters of a stagnant pond. Haeckel was a Darwinian extremist and I take his cynical utterance to be the absolute ultimate of the animal theory of man.

But man will not accept any theory of materialism and animalism offered to him in explanation of himself and of his life in this world. Man knows that he is man, no matter what the biologists say. "There are more things in heaven and earth, Horatio, than are dreamt of in your philosophy," says Hamlet. And there are more things in the heart and soul of man than are named and numbered, described, defined, analyzed and synthesized, in the works of Darwin and Haeckel and Freud. The evolutionists go to the animals to learn about man. Why not go to man to learn about man? Scientists, of the materialistic stripe, are so intent upon fossils, fish, serpents, simians, alleged ante-cedents of man, that they have no eyes for man himself. "I sought Thee and I found Thee not because I sought Thee without; again I sought Thee and found Thee because I sought Thee within," says St. Augustine, speaking of God. These modern materialists are so sure there is no God that they don't even look for Him, without or within. But they do look for man and some one should convey to them the elementary information that the place to look for man is in man, not in rocks, or pools of slime, not in the depths of the sea or the heart of the jungle; not in laboratories or test tubes, not in vats of saline solution; not in protoplasm, atoms, molecules, ions, electrons, but in man.

They themselves insist that man has been in the making for countless ages, and that all the forces in the universe have been in labor to produce man. Very well then, why not look at the finished product? Don't ask the rocks, don't ask the amoeba, don't ask the tadpole, or the walrus, or the wolf, or the orangoutang. Ask the *Man*: What are you? What do you make of yourself?

And man will tell them. I don't mean merely man the philoso-pher, or man the theologian. I would not send skeptical enquirers to Aristotle or Immanuel Kant or Spinoza or Thomas Aquinas. These were professional philosophers; scientists are suspicious of philosophers—suspicious and perhaps jealous. So jealous that they are forever trespassing out of their own field of science into the field of philosophy.

But if not to philosophers, why not to the prophets, the seers, the poets? These dig their material out of the heart of man. There is David and Solomon, and the writer of Job, and Isaias and John the Divine, and Paul and Augustine and à Kempis and Dante and Shakespeare (there is ten thousand times more knowledge of man in Shakespeare than in Immanuel Kant) and Wordsworth and Coleridge and Conrad and Masefield.

Above all, first of all, if the materialists could overcome their prejudices, their narrow notion that man is to be studied in the field and the laboratory but not in his own heart, I would send them to our Lord and Savior Jesus Christ. "He knew what was in man and needed not that any man should tell Him."

The poets and prophets know man because like the pope in Browning's "The Ring and the Book" (a superb revelation, by the way, of human nature) they "have studied many hearts beginning with their own." Ask them and they will answer: "We don't know all about man: the subject is vast, profound, illimitable. Man is a world in himself; to study man is to study the world. He is a combination of all the forces that have been at work in this mysterious universe since the dawn of time; to understand him would be to know the universe. We don't know man thoroughly. But we do know enough about man to laugh at the ridiculous and obscene idea that man is only a highly organized intricately constructed animal. If that were all, man could be as content as a cow; no more introspective than a hippopotamus soaking at his ease in the tepid waters of a tropical pool. If he were only an animal he would experience no more remorse for his sins than a tiger that has killed a gazelle. If he were only an animal, that question—"What's It All About?"—would not so much as occur to him. The fact that he asks it and cannot rest content until he answers it is the best evidence that there is something in the depths of his being that goads him like a gadfly, that makes him discontented with what he has and what he sees, that tells him he was not born to die; something that not only stings him and tortures him but that lifts him up to ecstasy, that enables him to fare forth— in the body or out of the body, he knows not—beyond the *flammantia moenia mundi*, the flaming ramparts and bastions that mark the edge of this world; something that tells him that he does not belong to this world but to another, and that his life on this planet is no more like the real life he is to live than the life of the embryo in the dark narrow confines of the womb is like life in the sunshine under the wide sky, surrounded on all sides by the wide horizon, surrounded but not confined because that wide horizon expands forever and forever.

And so we come upon the answer to the question with which we commenced, "What Is It All About?" Why all these torturing thoughts at the roots of the mind of man? Why all these longings and expectations of a life beyond life? Why these "unsearchable groanings of man's heart"? There must be meaning in the incessant repetition of the drama of life, the drama that neither Sophocles nor Shakespeare could write, try as they would. And what *is* that meaning? Why do we labor and strive and grieve and struggle? Why are we so tempted? Why do we sin? When we sin, why can we not be happy? Why do we repent and suffer agonies of remorse? These and a thousand more questions arising in the human soul are the material of which all literature, poetry, drama, fiction (fiction I have said which if it be literature is not fiction), all art and music, are composed. Religion deals with these questions and answers them. All human experiences, sufferings, joys, problems—though not the essential substance of religion—are taken into account by religion. Religion corroborates the answer given by literature and art and philosophy.

This life is not so much life as a prelude to life. If there were no other life but this, this life would be horrible, inexplicable, indefensible, inexcusable. The only explanation and justification of this life is the other life. This life without the other would be like one hemisphere without the other. This hemisphere is in the dark, the other in the light. To die is not to go from darkness to deeper darkness, but from darkness to light. "Out of the shadows and the images into the light."

"What then, finally, is this life all about?" It's about the other life, the true life, immortal life.

Chapter 33

Academic Freedom

"ACADEMIC FREEDOM" is a fine phrase. It sounds learned and brave and bold and adventurous, and all that. When, a generation or two ago, American colleges were aping the German system, they imported from what was then held to be the most learned nation in the world, the principle of *Absolute Academic Freedom*. That principle may be surmised from such statements of it as these:

In 1898 Professor G. Kaufmann writing on "Freedom of Teaching in the German Universities" said, "There must be no barriers to the freedom of a univerisity teacher except those of his own instinct for the truth."

And Professor Friedrich Paulsen wrote, "No thought can be commanded or forbidden to the academic teacher or his students."

And Adolf Harnack: "In regard to research and knowledge, there must be unlimited freedom." He saw the latent possibility of danger, but he insisted: "the fear that unlimited academic freedom throws open the door to serious error should not in the least deter us from it, for the most serious error of all is the opinion that man should not enjoy perfect freedom."

Also recognizing the danger, Professor Kaufmann added to the statement I have quoted from him, "Whatever the academic teacher produces from his subjective veracity must be inviolable: he may proclaim it as truth, regardless of consequences."

In 1914, as soon as the war drums commenced to roll, most of those advocates of perfect intellectual liberty swallowed their words. But in those dear dread days beyond recall academic freedom was a brave bold slogan, and the pick of American scholars came back from Europe proclaiming it. It is odd and tragic that on this side of the water, the nabobs of higher education are still mouthing the phrase "Academic Freedom."

In 1923 President Nicholas Murray Butler of Columbia University said: "No professor of ours is or ever has been under any restrictions save those which he puts upon himself by reason of good morals and good manners. Columbia has through a long and honorable history lived up to the highest ideals of freedom to seek the truth and freedom to teach."

President Lowell, former president of Harvard, answered a statement of Bertrand Russell to the effect that English universities were freer than American. He said: "At Oxford not long ago, if I am right, a student's publication *The New Oxford,* was suppressed on account of remarks that it contained. Nothing of the kind has, I believe, occurred here in the memory of man. During the war, you lost your fellowship at Cambridge on account of your opinions. No such thing happened at Harvard. Harvard has stood, and will stand for the fullest academic freedom." At that time also, President Hopkins of Darmouth declared that even "pernicious" doctrines may be taught to college boys and girls provided "like access be not denied to other points of view."

There is plenty of evidence—too much—that the professors have taken very seriously the *carte blanche* handed them by the prexies. One professor exercising his prerogative of saying whatever his instinct for the truth dictated, says, speaking of marriage, "Free sex intercourse is the highly moral product of a healthy social organism."

And another: "Monogamy, with its lifelong hold on both parties, is incompatible with personal freedom"; and since divorce entails expense, he adds, "It is better to have no marriage ceremony at all and simply have those who love each other live together as husband and wife as long as they agree with each other."

That suggestion reminds me of a quaint conceit of Cosmo Hamilton, who said in debate with G. K. Chesterton: "Marriage is made not in heaven but on the top of a tram, or in a canoe on a placid stream, or during a walk in the woods, when the boy says 'Will you marry me?' and the girl answers 'I will.'" That, said he, "is the marriage, and any demand that it be recorded in a magistrate's office or at city hall or in a church is tyranny."

Another professor says, "Psychologically, institutional religion is sex perversion."

A reference book used in many colleges, Metchnikoff's *Nature of Man,* explains that "man is a kind of miscarriage of the ape."

And another: "Jesus, in condoning the offense of the woman taken in adultery, set the stamp of His approval upon sexual relations based on mere inclination."

Another quotes with approbation the dictum of Nietzsche: "Morality is the greatest enemy of life."

An ex-professor in a girls' college, now writing for a newspaper syndicate, declares dogmatically: "All gods are the creation of the human imagination. There never has been any divine revelation and never will be. No extant moral code, not even that derived from the Bible, possesses divine authority. Conscience is nothing more than the product of group opinion."

And another professor: "All crimes are produced by various chemicals called hormones which are manufactured by the different glands."

And again Metchnikoff: "Evolution knows nothing of free will, all our actions are the necessary outcome of chemical processes."

A professor of Sociology ridicules the idea that a criminal is a free moral agent responsible for his crime, and a college reference book specifies: "Suppose a tramp has murdered a child on the highway, has robbed her of a few coppers and has thrown her body in the ditch. Do you mean to say he is not to blame and not be punished? Yes, I mean to say just that."

But enough. Any one familiar with the current trend in college sociology, ethics, criminology, psychology, biology must be aware that a thousand such mad statements as these could be assembled. In accordance with the claims of absolute academic freedom, one may teach Socialism, Communism, Atheism; universal skepticism, or philosophic nihilism; the superiority of Paganism over Christianity; the advantage of polygamy over monogamy; the desirability of monarchy rather than democracy or, as Marx did, anarchy as the ultimate perfection. A professor may teach today a subversive opinion that he will abandon tomorrow. Abusing the advantage of having young men and young women when they are in their most receptive and impressionable years, he may skillfully and powerfully indoctrinate them with views, which, after his students have graduated and are beyond his reach, he may abandon as absurd. The implications of the theory of absolute academic freedom are infinite.

Many years ago a group of twenty-six alumni of Amherst, laying down a program for a liberal college said: "A liberal college should give the student the beautiful experience of exposure to conflicting viewpoints, and train him to accept no opinion until he has made it his own by careful examination and critical weighing of the best possible evidence." I submit that this is pure nonsense. Anybody who knows the intellectual caliber of undergraduates in American colleges, is aware that they are quite incapable of "carefully examining and critically weighing the best possible evidence." By the very nature of the case, a student who takes up a dozen or score of subjects in a four years' college course can have only a smattering of them when he graduates. To tell him that he must not accept anything until he has made it his own by a critical investigation is asking something of which the student is incapable intellectually. Indeed, his professors are likewise incapable of it. They study for a lifetime and then disagree with one another. When professors disagree, shall the student decide? You might as well ask him to decide between Newton and Einstein.

A little preaching of intellectual humility would do the student more good than all this foolish flattery. The student should be told: "You don't know how to think until you come to college. Unless you are the rare exception you won't know how to think when you leave. So don't let anyone flatter you with the notion that you have the critical faculty of deciding for yourself and don't let any twenty-six alumni, or twenty-six hundred alumni, deceive you with the statement that you, an undergraduate, even after the 'beautiful experience of exposure to conflicting viewpoints,' will be able to make an opinion your own by 'careful investigation and critical weighing of the evidence.' My dear boy, it cannot be done."

Back in the early years of this century the celebrated Dr. Osler of Johns Hopkins gave a lecture at Harvard on "Immortality." The plan of the lecture was to pass in review the supreme masters of thought in all ages: Aristotle, Plato, Seneca, Epictetus, Cicero, Maimonides, Mohammed, Augustine, Aquinas, Erasmus, Locke, Hume, Kant, the Bible, the Rig-Veda, the Zend Avesta, and other authorities, Christian and non-Christian, conservative and radical, of believers and unbelievers, orthodox and infidel. In the end Dr. Osler professed himself agnostic on the subject of Immortality. What wonder. No man can sit in judgment on the truth or error in the mind of all the thinkers of the human race. And if no man can do it, no boy or girl can do it. The idea of dishing up to college students all kinds of mental pabulum, good and bad, true and false, healthful and unhealthful is excellent if you wish to drug the students or poison them. But if the purpose of education is to feed the mind, not suffocate it, absolute academic freedom is nonsense and damnable dangerous nonsense.

And this is the nonsense that the Catholic Church has learned to reject. She claims to have divine revelation and direct relationship with the Holy Spirit. But she doesn't need any supernatural light to show her that it is a mad thing to bewilder the minds of students and demoralize them because of stupid devotion to a slogan, "Academic Freedom." Having common sense, the Church has avoided that pitfall, that bog, that sea of sticky slime in which the modern mastodon of university education is now caught and in which it is feebly floundering before it becomes entirely and inextricably submerged.

Chapter 34

Life and Literature

IN HIS address to the players, Prince Hamlet says "the purpose of playing . . . both at the first and now, was and is, to hold as 'twere the mirror up to nature." What he says of play-acting—the drama—I think we may say of literature. The purpose of literature is to hold the mirror up to nature. But the supreme poet-dramatist most certainly did not mean that drama should present to the spectator or literature to the reader only the sort of reflection that we get in a mirror. Almost every mirror lies to us: it flatters or it libels; it makes us more handsome than we are or more ugly; it idealizes or caricatures. It is a rare mirror indeed that shows the human countenance precisely as it is. And by the same token it is a rare play or poem or piece of prose that shows man or nature or life just as it is.

Besides, even if the mirror be perfect, it still can give us only a superficial reflection. A mirror, like a photograph, does not interpret spirit, personality, character. For that you need an artist. The reason a portrait painter asks so many sittings is that he must have time to study not so much the face as the physiognomy. He must see back of the eyes, behind the skin. If he is an artist indeed he can read the soul of the man who sits to him, capture that soul and put it on the canvas. In the finished portrait you see what the mirror or the photograph cannot tell; what perhaps the man himself did not know was in him, something that may perhaps startle and shock him when he sees it. Hurrell Froude says that when John Henry Newman preached to the young men at Oxford "He revealed ourselves to ourselves and the revelation startled us." There you have the mark of a great preacher; it is a revelation of man to himself. And there too is the touchstone of great art or great literature. It probes deep, it brings up truth from hidden corners of the heart and soul; it reveals that truth to us, and the revelation startles or shocks or thrills us, exalts, depresses, elates or appals us—at any rate deeply moves us.

Literature reveals man to man, and doing so it reveals the world and life to man. For what we call "the world," is after all nothing else but man. Man is the world, and the world is man. The world without man, is nothing. Stars, planets, solar universes are important only if they help man to understand himself. We look through the telescope to see ourselves. And so of the microscope. Of what interest is a bug or a germ or a pinpoint of protoplasm on a slab of glass unless somehow, directly or indirectly, it explains something to man? "The proper study of mankind is man," says the poet. The only study of mankind is man, at least as far as the natural universe is concerned. When we transcend the natural universe and come to the supernatural, especially to the Absolute Supernatural which is God, we still scrutinize God, so to speak, primarily because the study of God is important to man. In fact we look to God to see man. *Noverim me, Noverim te,* says St. Augustine. May I know myself and may I know thee, and in this matter as in a thousand others, St. Augustine is in advance of Socrates who said to man "Know thyself," unless you contend that Socrates knew that man could not know himself unless he knew God.

We have come a long distance from the mirror and the photograph. What we are seeking is an answer to the question: "What is the relationship of literature to life?" Literature, or drama, or music or any other art has for its purpose the revelation of man to man, the revelation of God to man, the interpretation to man of the meaning of his life on this whirling, bewildering, dizzying globe. I find in *A Philosophy of Literature,* by Brother Azarias, published in Philadelphia 80 years ago, this significant, and I think, eloquent passage:

"Man, as we now find him, is restless, ill satisfied with himself, seldom content with the sphere in which his duties lie, and always looking above and beyond, dreaming of ideal worlds and ideal situations, in which he loves to forget the smoke and dust, the thorny paths and stony roads, through which he moves in his every-day existence. Literature fosters and partially satisfies this craving of his nature. It bears him into the regions of the sublime, the beautiful, the marvelous; and his soul rejoices in the transfer. Deep in the recesses of his heart there resound vague whisperings, the exact import of which fancy seems incompetent to catch—spectres of thought to which imagination has been unable to give shape or hue; weak impulses, whither tending he cannot tell."

To forget the smoke and dust, to seek the sublime, the beautiful, the marvelous, to look above and beyond, to crave ideal worlds and ideal situations, all this is laughed at as an illusion by most modern writers. In consequence they remain only scribblers, at best literary craftsmen. They are not worthy of the name "author" for an author is a creator. The one who ridicules or repudiates the spiritual aspirations of man must remain only a reporter like some newly graduated collegian who for a wage rushes hither and thither, to a fire, to the scene of a murder, to a wrecked train, to a criminal court, to an execution, to a prizefight or a football game; writes it down, or telephones it in to his editor. He tells us what he sees, but what he sees is just what anyone would see who happened to be there. If, however, an occasional rare reporter tells us what we would *not* see, *could* not see even if we were eyewitnesses; if he reports a murder-trial or an electrocution, or even some pathetic sordid event like what the dwellers in tenements used to call a "dispossess," but reports it so that we see behind, below, above the actual incident; if he gives us what a musician would call the undertones and the overtones, so that the pathos or the tragedy or perhaps the sardonic or the ironic humor of the event stirs our imagination, grips the heart, reveals some hidden aspect of human nature that we had never suspected or known, or realized before—then the journalistic stint may turn out to be a bit of literature.

But if the reporter discloses what the human eye could not see, some phase or feature of the episode that could not be caught by even the most candid camera, he must have dug it out of his own heart. In his heart he found it, from the heart he projected it into the heart of the victim, or the criminal or the actor, or the sufferer in the drama of daily life; and then by the means of literary magic, the wizardry of words, he projects into our hearts what he first tore out of his own. That is literature, not a bald presentation of life but a manifestation, an interpretation, a revelation.

But no man can reveal me to myself or my life to myself unless he has me in his heart. "Look into thy heart . . . and write," said a wise old counsellor. Well, where else could he look? He cannot look into my heart. There is an old phrase about the "inscrutable oriental mind." Oriental or occidental the mind of man is inscrutable and the depths of his heart unfathomable. "*Secretum meum mihi*," my secret is my own. No man can break down the barrier of my inscrutability. No man but the Judge of the living and the dead. Of Jesus Christ it is said in the Gospel, "He needed not that any should give testimony of man: for he knew what was in man." Of no other man may that be said without grave qualification. No man knows what is in man. No man knows even the specimen of man that is nearest and most familiar— himself. I know myself, I read my own heart, with faltering and uncertainty. I am a riddle to myself, and shall some stranger come along and read me? I do not "wear my heart on my sleeve for daws to peck at." Nor is there a window to my heart through which the curious may look as physicians look through a window into the stomach of a guinea pig. "Will you play upon this pipe?" says Hamlet to Guildenstern, handing him a "recorder" or as we should say a flageolet. "My lord, I cannot," says Guildenstern; and after some trifling with the stupid fellow sent by the king to spy upon him, Hamlet cries out with indignation: "You would play upon me; you would seem to know my stops; you would pluck out the heart of my mystery; you would sound me from my lowest note to the top of my compass . . ." 'Sblood, do you think I am easier to be played on than a pipe? Call me what instrument you will, though you can fret me, yet you cannot play upon me."

But the marvel and the miracle about the man of genius is that he can and does play upon our heart strings like Paganini upon the violin. The unknown author I have already quoted says, "Literature appeals to the senses in their widest range, from the sphere of simple delight, such as is afforded by the fable or the nursery tale . . . through all phases of passion, to the intense strain of terror or pity inspired by tragedy. It moves the reader to tears; it excites him to mirth and laughter; and often, while professing only to please, it initiates him into all the secrets of the heart."

Now the fact is, the incredible mystical fact, that the whole world *is* in one man's heart. Man is, as we say, "a microcosm," a world in little. All men who ever lived, the highest, the noblest, the meanest, and the most loathsome, are in me. In every man is the saint and the criminal, the martyr and the murderer, the dull, stupid, plodding, phlegmatic peasant and the poet who spurns the earth and soars into the empyrean like the skylark:

> Higher still and higher
> From the cloud thou springest
> Like a cloud of fire
> The deep blue thou wingest
> And singing still dost soar,
> And soaring ever singest.

Shelley might have been describing himself the poet, or an artist, or a musician, or any other man of genius, or in fact any reader to whom those lines appeal, because the reader could not enjoy the lines unless he had in himself some share of the poet's—or the skylark's—lofty aspiration.

"Realists," as they love to call themselves, especially modern realists in literature and in the drama, do not understand this higher nature in man. They look upon him as a beast, an especially stupid, vicious, sordid species of beast. Indeed to judge from some of the popular fiction of the day, one might imagine that the writers of it were but elaborating upon the statement of one of the characters (Franz Moor) in Schiller's play *Die Rauber,* who says: "Man is made of filth and for a time wades in filth, till at last he is buried and fouls the boots of his own posterity. Such is . . . the filthy circle of human fate." Many a recent "best seller" itself as well as the characters it contains might be described in those words.

It would be easy to permit oneself to grow indignant over this rank "realism," but it is sufficient to say that "realists" simply do not know man. We who loathe what is called "realism" do not criticize Zola or Maxim Gorki or James Joyce or James T. Farrell because they irritate us or nauseate us, though of course they do. We merely say that their writings are not literature and cannot be literature because they do not know the material out of which literature is made, the heart and mind and soul of man. "Nothing will live that is written in a perverse spirit," says John Lancaster Spalding. No, nor will anything live that is written in ignorance of the complete nature of man. Was it Matthew Arnold who said that the artist is one who "sees life steadily and sees it whole"? The realists see life—the life of man—unsteadily, and they do not see it whole. Until they do, they will never write literature. They are afflicted by some strange mental and spiritual malady that blinds them to what is beautiful and lets them see only what is ugly. But the world and man and life are not all ugly. The sun has spots but the sun is not all spots. There are sewers beneath the surface in every great city, but no great city is all sewers. There is disease in the body politic and the body social, but the body is not all disease.

There is a spark that animates this dust, there is a flame and a fire within this clay. Man is, in one aspect, "of the earth earthy," but the paradox, the mystery, and incidentally the torture, is that he is at the one same time unearthly, a spirit, a soul, a god. "Have I not said ye are gods?" is a line from the Old Testament quoted by Jesus Himself in the New. "Man," says Arthur Machen, "is not the creature of the drawing room or of the stock exchange but a lonely awful soul confronted by the source of all souls." True! and human life is not eating and drinking, buying and selling, investing, gambling, exulting in the upturn of the market, desponding at its collapse; and by the same token—most modern novelists notwithstanding—life is not all flirting, playing at love, as if love were a game, cheating at the game of love, betraying and outraging love. Life does not consist in what St. Augustine calls "polluting the pure stream of love with the sewage of lust." When a novelist or a dramatist in what is commonly but falsely called a "love story" leads two human souls to the brink of moral disaster and, nine times out of ten, pushes them over into the abyss of carnal sin, and repeats the process *ad lib* and *ad nauseam* in a score of successive novels or a hundred, knowing not what else to do with his male and female puppets except to make them sin, he may think that he has sounded the depths of love and exhausted its possibilities, but the chances are that he has never so much as caught a hasty glimpse of the nature and the meaning of love.

As of love, so of life. There was, some years ago, a play called *Design for Living*. But if we are to judge from the literary product that is glutting the book market and overflowing into the drug stores (perhaps it is the most dangerous drug in the drug store) there would seem to be but one design for living known to contemporary novelists. That one design is repeated with deadly monotony like a design in wallpaper or like the blinking of electric signs, in and out, on and off, in and out, on and off, until the eye is paralyzed and the brain benumbed.

Meanwhile a world of excellent literary material exists all around and above us. A novelist with eyes to see could pick it out of the air in front of his face; if his spiritual olfactory nerve were sensitive he could smell life in the atmosphere; if his finger tips were delicate he could feel the touch of life by merely holding out his hand. I venture to say much the same thing about drama. We are asked to read novels, as we are asked to see on the stage, a sickening reiteration of the same superficialities, or, if the tale or the plot be more serious, the same sordidness, as if there were nothing in life but adultery and fornication, matrimonial infidelity, intrigue, deceit, treachery, violence. One might imagine that the writers of fiction gather their material from clinics for Freudian diseases, or from the pages of the tabloid newspapers. I think they do. But meanwhile all the genuine pathos, the true deep tragedy of human life; all the genuine heartache, the hopes, the longings, the dejection of the human soul and its exaltation, its despondency and its ecstasy, the "unspeakable groanings of the spirit," as St. Paul calls them; the divine hunger and thirst; the storming of the gate of heaven by the invincible soul of man; his assault upon the battlements of the celestial world with no weapons but his hope, his faith, his love—all these things go unrecorded, even unrecognized, by the writers of the day.

In a word, the fatal fault in fiction as in drama is that it is a mirror, a photograph of Broadway, of Hollywood, of Park Avenue, of Mayfair, of the Boulevards, of Montmartre, or when it attempts something a bit different, a chronicle of politics or a sociological pamphlet done in fiction form.

We have much cheap and pseudo-humorous talk nowadays about "The Facts of Life," and the presumption seems to be that we the orthodox, we the so-called conservatives, are in a conspiracy to conceal the facts of life. But what we want above all things else is the facts of life, not in the silly sense in which the phrase is commonly used but in its deepest and widest meaning. The facts of life are in our Bible. The Old Testament and the New are imperishable masterpieces of literature largely because they speak frankly and powerfully the facts of life. Our philosophy, our theology, our sermons, the lives of the saints, our books of moral and ascetical doctrine, are packed and jammed with the facts of life. There is more about the facts of life in the *Confessions* of St. Augustine, in the *Dialogue* of St. Catherine of Siena, and in the sermons of St. Bernard and of Cardinal Newman, than in a half hundred Bernard Shaws or Henrik Ibsens, D. H. Lawrences, in Chekhov or Dostoievsky; or even in the formidable trilogy and tetralogy of Sigrid Undset.

We are not afraid of life or the facts of life. Nor for that matter of what comes after life: Death, Judgment, Heaven, Hell. Without those "Four Last Things" as a background, no literature can be great, because without them no human life is significant. What we dislike and reprobate is the "counterfeit presentment" of life, using the phrase in another sense than that of Shakespeare, the faking of life, the lying about life, the distortion of life, the refusal to look at life whole and to tell of life as it is.

And there, if you would know is the reason why we think that the literature of the day is largely either froth or filth. It is dishonest about life, insincere, evasive, not courageous, not searching, not comprehensive, not illuminating. But we still cherish the hope that the day will come when literature once again may turn to life, and present not a superficial photograph of life, but a penetrating and therefore authentic exposition of life at its very depths. When that day comes we shall have literature that is literature, literature that *is* life.

Chapter 35

The Marks of An Educated Man

WHAT is it to be educated? Are we an educated people? Are we getting adequate returns for our investment in education? If a banker or manufacturer or merchant put as much capital and labor and thought and care into a money-making project and got no better results in his line than educators do in theirs, would he continually send good money after bad? If the coach of a college team produced no better athletes than the professors produced scholars, would he remain the idol of the under-graduates and the toast of the alumni? Connie Mack, master-mind at the national game, used to take a group of raw "bushers," teach them "inside baseball" and win world's championships with them. Knute Rockne performed the even greater miracle of making a relatively small mid-western college unbeatable at football. In a different art, Leopold Auer produced in succession such virtuosi as Efram Zimbalist, Mischa Elman and Jascha Heifetz. Is there, then, anything unfair in the demand that a vast, expensive, elaborately equipped educational system should get conspicuously good results?

There are more than three million students enrolled in colleges, universities and professional schools in the United States, to say nothing of the many more millions of children in the primary and grammar grades and in the secondary schools. One person in every 100 of the entire population is receiving what is called euphemistically "higher education." Do we get adequate results?

A generation ago Abraham Flexner in his provocative work

Universities declared roundly that most college students amongst us are "not being educated at all"; and that even of those who attend the best accredited institutions of learning "there is no certainty that they have been properly prepared or that they are pursuing a course that deserves to be called a liberal education." Apparently fearful of being considered too exacting or unfair he explained, "I have spared no effort to obtain the facts and to submit my views in advance to competent criticism." Thirty professors or administrators in America and Europe (he wrote of Germany and England also) read his text carefully and commented on it freely. He does not claim that all of them accept his views, but it seems that many of them in America think as meanly as he of our system of education, and one of them, a dean of Columbia college makes the drastic statement, "I am convinced that the youth of college age are as immature morally and as crude socially as they are undeveloped intellectually."

So, what is an educated person and what are the marks by which we shall know him?

First, it seems to me, the educated man should know how to think. Is it silly to say so? I am not sure. I have sat with too many college men on railroad trains and planes, at golf clubs, at banquets, at private dinners; I have promenaded back and forth interminably on the decks of ocean liners with them and have listened dutifully, though often painfully, while they uttered what they called their convictions, but which were really emotions, prejudices, snap judgments. One comes to realize that there are certain questions—and they are very many—on which great numbers of "educated" men apparently cannot think dispassionately. For example, Freemasonry, religion in the public schools, the Jewish question or any phase of it, the Catholic Church, justice to the black man, a Catholic for President, Christian Science, Capitalism, Communism. But why continue? Virtually all topics of daily conversation are discussed without logic, with bias, emotion and passion.

Take the question of corrupt politics. If one delivers a public discourse, or even makes a remark in private conversation about "graft," he will stir up some such irrelevant observation as that "the other fellows are just as bad"; or "New York is no worse than Philadelphia, and not so bad as Chicago"; or "Reformers are the worst of all crooks"; or "The organization is kind to the poor"; or "Politics is politics and they don't go into politics for their health." All these observations may be true, but what have they to do with the essence of the matter, the sin and the crime of "graft"?

Or take the Jewish question. Hilaire Belloc in his work *The Jews,* closes his preface with this protestation: "I will conclude by asking my Jewish, as well as my non-Jewish, readers to observe that I have left out every allusion and every element of mere recrimination . . . I have left out everything of the kind because, though one can always rouse interest in this way, it excites enmity between the opposing parties. I could have made the book far stronger as a piece of polemic and indefinitely more amusing as a piece of record, but I have not written it as a piece of polemic or as a piece of record. I have written it as an attempt at justice."

But he predicts that no one, Jew or non-Jew, will be satisfied with the treatise. He might have added that very few would even admit his sincerity. Years afterwards he said that though the book was widely read it was almost as widely attacked. It would not be so painful if only the incurably ignorant, the habitually passionate, refused to discuss the Jews patiently and temperately, but the tragedy is that *educated* persons cannot see the simple proposition that no matter what may be the faults of any race, that race should not be persecuted.

Come to a second mark of the educated man. He must be able as St. Augustine says "to distinguish the charlatanism of words from the reality of things." The charlatanism of words! I have sat at a lecture delivered by a tall handsome speaker of impressive if not magnetic personality, and after some ten or fifteen minutes of close and sympathetic attention I have been compelled to ask myself, "Now just what is it all about?" That lecture was a curious phenomenon. Every word had a meaning. The lecture was delivered with sonority and even with an air of magnificence. But though the words had a meaning, the discourse as a whole had none. It was an odd performance, and I expected the hearers to be either puzzled or amused. But on all sides as we left the hall we heard enthusiastic commendation and no confession of bewilderment. Yet the hearers were all "educated." Is this what their education had done for them—left them unable to distinguish sound from sense?

We are inclined to pride ourselves on the fact that nowadays no one can fool us with grandiose, vociferous oratory. That style is definitely obsolete. But another equally bad style has taken its place. We seem to have rejected one form of charlatanry only to be victimized by another. The main question is whether a people who permit themselves to be fooled with oratorical charlatanry, loud or soft, can be called an educated people.

A third mark of an educated man is tolerance. Tolerance, it seems to me, is a quality of the mind rather than of the heart. It is mental more than moral. The intolerant are not inhuman. They are unintelligent. If you were to say to a member of the Ku-Klux-Klan: "Surely, you cannot believe in the alleged Knight of Columbus oath. You don't really imagine that Patrick Kelly, your next door neighbor, who gives you a cheery 'Good Morning,' walks with you to work, loans you his lawnmower and borrows your screwdriver, would cut your throat and disembowel you upon the command of the Pope!" What would he answer? He would probably say Patrick Kelly my Catholic neighbor would not murder me and rape my wife—not as Patrick Kelly! "But as a Knight of Columbus and a minion of the Pope, I don't know what he might do." And yet the members of the Klan are the product of the American educational system.

An educated man should be a bit of a philosopher. He need not have read all the philosophies—heaven help him—nor have made his analysis and synthesis of every system from Aristotle's to Bergson's. But he ought to have a bowing acquaintance with the principal efforts that have been made to read the riddle of the universe, and he ought to know enough not to be scornful of any system of thought elaborated by the world's great masters of wisdom. Yet Will Durant omitted a thousand years of philosophy on the pretext that it was beneath notice. But a thousand years of thought is never unworthy of notice. When Carlyle called Dante "the voice of ten silent centuries," he must have been straining after an epigram, or suffering delusions about the "dark ages." There are no ten silent centuries. The truth is, of course, that Durant merely disliked Scholasticism, so he left it out of his *Story of Philosophy*. But an educated man must be interested even in what he dislikes. He remembers *nil humani alienum*. All things human are of interest to him. And not the least of things human is human thought.

An educated man should have some grasp of what is called a philosophy of life. In the suggestive and stimulating volume to which I have already referred, Abraham Flexner speaks of "a Whitehead or an Eddington trying to make out what it all means." Whether one is Whitehead, an Eddington or even a plain John Smith, he should do just that—try to find out what it all means. If a policeman accosts a man in the street and asks him, "Who are you, what are you doing here, and where are you going," the fellow must make some plausible reply. If he returns an "I don't know" he will be asked to step around to the station house or more likely to the psychopathic ward. But in the world of what passes for learning, men seem to take pride in saying that they don't know who or what they are, why they came to this planet, what they are doing here, and where they are going.

An educated man should have a modicum of culture. A college graduate must have started with at least a rudimentary faculty for the appreciation of art and music and literature. Nature endows every child born into the world with some slight feeling for poetry. If that rudimentary faculty has remained undeveloped while the child has grown and waxed strong and gone through school and college, isn't the net result of education imperfect? Didn't Herbert Spencer define education as "preparation for a complete life"? And is a life complete in which art and music and poetry have no place? Charles Darwin wrote in his *Autobiography* that after long application to biology and anthropology he lost his taste for literature. He had been so long engaged exclusively in deducing general theories from specific facts that Shakespeare, for example, no longer appealed to him. A man who ceases to appreciate Shakespeare has to a degree succeeded in uneducating himself.

Yes, there should be a feeling for high poetry and fine music and noble drama. There should even be a kind of hankering and a hunger of the soul for the touch of mysticism that is in all true art. I know it sounds ridiculous nowadays in America to argue that education involves culture. But the older generation and the younger will not agree as to why it is ridiculous. The old school will think the argument ridiculous because supererogatory. The younger generation who have been brought up on "science" will think the demand for culture ridiculous because culture is to them a mere luxury or a superfluity or an excrescence indicative of decadence. They have "science"—what need have they of art?

The passing mention of mysticism may serve to introduce my final mark of an educated man—final not because it concludes the subject but because I must make an end. The educated man must have a religion. I once heard the president of a state university say to the undergraduates: "Young men, young women, be religious. A person without religion is diseased, debased, degenerate." The pronouncement was startling, especially so in view of the fact that on the platform behind the president were a dozen or a score of atheist professors. Were the professors not educated men? Even at the risk of writing myself down a fanatic, I will not dodge that question. The atheist is not educated.

But let us understand what we mean in this instance by religion. I use the word just now in its minimum sense. And I venture to say of education what Arthur Machen (in *Hieroglyphics*) says of literary talent. You cannot have it unless you believe in the eternal truths and—what is more important—*feel* them as realities. Machen says that literature is the expression of Catholic dogma, but he adds: "Don't imagine that you can improve your literary chances by subscribing to the Catechism or the decrees of the Council of Trent. But unless you have assimilated the dogmas— the eternal truths on which these things rest . . . you never can write literature." You must realize, he continues, "that man is not the creature of the drawing room or the Stock Exchange, but a lonely soul, confronted by the Source of all souls." Earlier in the same volume he speaks of "the ecstasy, rapture, adoration, awe, mystery, sense of the unknown, desire for the unknown," which differentiates literature from "the mass of stuff which is not literature."

What a writer of literature must possess, the educated man must not lack. He must feel the mystery at the heart of the universe, the mystery in a blade of grass, a drop of water, or as Walt Whitman says, the mystery in a hair on the back of his hand. With infinite mysteries before his eyes and under his feet and over his head, the educated man will not be flippant. He will not scoff. He will be reverent. He will walk softly and speak gently as though the whole world were a sanctuary, as indeed it is.

Chapter 36

Why Must the Innocent Suffer?

IN RELIGION, as in all other departments of human life, complete intellectual honesty is indispensable. There is scarcely any worse sin than refusal to see and to confess the truth. So, in considering the question which concerns us in this chapter, "Why Must the Innocent Suffer?," we would best commence by admitting that we do not know. That is to say, we do not know, if to know means to comprehend. "We know in part, and we prophesy in part," says St. Paul; and he adds, "We see now through a glass in a dark manner." We see not as one looking at a physical object in full sunlight, but like one groping in gloom. If anyone tells you that to him the mysteries of religion are as plain as A.B.C. you may put him down as a charlatan. Once in my life I heard a man say, "Predestination is no mystery to me." "Wonderful," said I, "you are more privileged that St. Thomas Acquinas, St. Augustine, or St. Paul. You must be a prophet and more than a prophet."

In the Catholic religion at least, mystery is recognized and emphasized. "What is a mystery?", asks the Catechism, and the answer is given: "A mystery is a truth that we cannot fully understand." That question and answer should appear in catechisms of science as well as of religion. If you don't understand, you don't understand. The poet said that if he understood a flower in the crannied wall, he would understand God. Religion has no monopoly of mystery. The whole universe is crammed with mystery. We have called it in the first pages of this book,

This Mysterious Universe. So, if a scientist declares that he will not accept religion because he refuses to recognize mystery, you may also put him down as a charlatan. There are as many scientific charlatans as theological charlatans, if not more.

So much by way of warning to those who expect a too precise answer to the question: "Why must the innocent suffer?" St. Augustine was held back from the Catholic Faith in his early days because, for one reason, he demanded, as one editor of the *Confessions* says, "a trenchant uncompromising answer" to his questions—"such an answer as young men love." Young or old, we all like to have unqualified answers to our questions, absolutely clear solutions to our problems. We feel balked and frustrated if we don't get them. But we have no right to expect them. We live in a world of shadows and images. Plato said so 2300 years ago; and another man of genius, not much short of Plato, Cardinal Newman, said that leaving this life for the next we pass "out of shadows and images into the light." Then and not until then shall we see face to face and know as we are known.

To come to the question: Why must good people who have never done harm suffer? Especially why must they suffer at the hands of the wicked? "Christ," we say, "is on the cross and Herod on the throne." There was blood on that throne, as on the Cross, but the blood on Herod's throne was other men's blood; the blood on the Cross of Christ was His own. Why does the man who spills the blood of others sit in comfort and honor, surrounded by fawning courtiers, while the Man who pours out His blood for His brethren hangs in agony and disgrace, surrounded by murderers and blasphemers? That's the question that confronts us. To answer it we should have to dig down deep to the roots of reason, and mount to the heights of revelation. Even then we shall not find the trenchant uncompromising answer that St. Augustine sought.

But one thing we do know: the Crucifixion of Our Lord is not only a fact but a symbol. From the day of that supreme tragedy until now the word "cross" has been used as a synonym for pain, physical and mental, for anguish of soul, for disappointment, shame, poverty, disgrace, dejection, despondency, the endurance of injustice, and, in brief, for suffering of every sort. Our Savior said: "If any man will come after me . . . let him take up his cross, and follow me"; "Where I am, there also shall my disciple be"; "Where I am," he says. But He was nailed to the cross. "Come down," said the scoffers, "Save Thyself." "Save Thyself and us," said the impenitent thief. But Christ came not down. He died on the cross. His disciples, therefore, must be nailed to the cross, perhaps remain upon it and die upon it. The disciple is not above the Master.

Christians are not alone in enduring the cross. Suffering is ubiquitous, perpetual, inevitable. In ancient days, as in our own, armies have swept across the face of the earth, making a shambles of one country after another and deliberately attempting to annihilate entire races and whole populations. When a Persian or a Macedonian or a Roman conqueror had won a victory, the vanquished were led away to be enslaved or slaughtered. Some few of them were guilty (if it be a guilty thing to defend one's own land), but for the most part they were poor innocent peasants, serfs, workingmen, no more responsible for the calamity that befell them than the French peasant, the Czechoslovakian mill worker, the Norwegian fisherman, the Hollander who grew tulips, milked the cows, made butter and cheese, was responsible for Hitler, or the 800 million sufferers behind the "Iron Curtain" were responsible for Lenin and Stalin. Peasants don't make wars. Politicians make wars. The politicians live, the peasants die. The guilty survive, the innocent perish.

Of old, victors in war led their victims captive, chained them in dungeons, left them to starve, or dragged them out to be devoured by beasts in the amphitheatre, to make a holiday for the mob. Nowadays, statesmen (save the mark!), attempt to do away with vanquished peoples by economic strangulation. Then statesmen on the other side turn the tables and wreak dire vengeance on the conquerors. The leaders of peoples—Fuehrers, Duces, Generals—strut around, proudly laden with medals, accept the idolatrous worship of the people, deliver truculent speeches, live in palaces, feed on the fat of the land. When they die, statues are erected to them. Around the statues crowds gather to listen to panegyrics, to scatter flowers, to shout and to sing, and to wish that another such conqueror might arise to lead them again to the battlefield for slaughter, as their fathers and grandfathers and forebears back to the beginning of history were led forth to slaughter.

For hundreds of years before William Wilberforce and Abraham Lincoln, the poor black man in the jungles of Africa who hadn't so much as known the existence of the white man and the white man's civilization (what irony there can be in that phrase "white man's civilization") were hunted down, whipped in droves like cattle from the forests to the sea, crowded into the stinking hold of slave ships, transported to another continent, sold like cattle, whipped as even cattle were not whipped. How much blood was spilled, what rivers of tears flowed, what poor simple hearts were broken, who can say, except perhaps the angels who record such things?

White men too, guilty of no worse crime than that of criticizing a corrupt government, or complaining of a tyrant, were taken from their homes, condemned with swift terrible injustice to the galleys, chained to an oar, whipped, clubbed, bruised, compelled to labor in blood and sweat, and perhaps left to drown like rats in the sinking hulk.

Others, a whole race of them guilty of no crime except that of being born of a despised blood, were driven under the lash to carry back-breaking burdens, to impossible tasks, building prodigious monuments to a king gone mad with vanity who feared that if there were no pyramid over his bones someone a thousand years later might forget that he was the illustrious Ptolemy or the ineffable Pharaoh.

But why attempt a comprehensive catalogue of the forms and varieties of torture inflicted upon the innocent by the wicked? Let these few specimens suffice in place of an encyclopedia of inhumanity.

But just one final word about man's suffering in our own day. We flatter ourselves that the world has grown more humane since the days of Darius, king of the Medes and Persians, or of Attila or of Tamerlane and Genghis Khan. But I am not so certain of it. Modern war with its mechanical contrivances for inflicting death at wholesale, and not only death—which might be a boon—but disfigurement, blinding a man, burning out his lungs with poison gas, or leaving him to grope about maimed for the rest of his days, or stretching him flat on his back with paralysis— this modern war is perhaps more cruel than the torture invented by fiendish Oriental despots in ancient days, or than the medieval rack and thumbscrew. Joan of Arc and Savonarola, I think, would have preferred burning alive rather than choking and agonizing with mustard gas. Certain authors of books with sadistic or ghoulish intent have dug into ancient records and have written histories of what our Federal Constitution calls "cruel and unusual punishment." But I cannot help wondering what the future historians will make of bombs dropped from the sky upon dwelling houses, churches, hospitals, kindergartens; or flame throwers on the field of battle, of torpedoes shot at merchant vessels, of mustard gas and perhaps of some still more ghastly means of torture newly invented to be inflicted upon people who had no say about the war and who are no more responsible for what England and France did to Germany, or what Germany has done to England and France, then they were responsible for the eruption of a volcano on the moon.

But now, after this hurried and inadequate résumé of some of the sufferings of the innocent because of the sins of the guilty, come the questions: "Why does not the Infinite Almighty God intervene? Is God indifferent? Is He a sphinx with an inscrutable expression on His countenance? A sphinx that hasn't lifted an eyebrow or moved a muscle in three thousand years, even though the white sands all about him have been sprinkled, drenched, saturated with human blood a hundred times over?

In the Old Testament we find the Psalmist taunting the heathen with the helplessness of their idols: "They have eyes and see not, ears and hear not: they have mouths and speak not." But it would seem that the heathen retorted that the God of David was equally impotent, and with some apparent reason, for the prophet king cries out:

> O God of vengeance, Lord,
> O God of vengeance, shine forth!
> Arise, judge of the earth,
> Render requital to the proud!
>
> How long, O Lord, shall the wicked—
> How long shall the wicked exult?
> They babble, they speak haughtily,
> All the workers of iniquity boast of themselves;
> They trample, O Lord, on thy people
> And afflict thine inheritance;
> They slay the widow and the stranger,
> And murder the fatherless,
> And they say: "The Lord sees it not;
> The God of Jacob regards it not."

But David has his answer to those who think God blind and deaf and dumb and helpless:

> Ye fools, when will ye be wise?
> He that fixed the ear, shall he not hear?
> He that formed the eye, shall he not see?
> He that gives sense to the nations, shall he not reprove?
> He that teaches men knowledge?

> The Lord knows the thoughts of men,
> That they are but as a breath . . .
>
> They assail the life of the righteous
> And condemn innocent blood.
> But the Lord shall be my high tower,
> And my God the rock of my refuge.
> He will bring down on them their own iniquity
> And by their own wickedness cut them off,
> He shall cut them off, the Lord our God.

Sometimes, as a matter of fact, God did punish the tyrant swiftly and visibly. In chapter seven of the second book of Machabees we read—if our squeamish stomachs can stand it—the detailed account of the tortures inflicted upon the seven brothers and their valiant mother by the incredible monster Antiochus. But if we go on to the second next chapter, we find described in equal detail the even more repulsive account of what happened to Antiochus. But, as St. Paul says, "I spare you."

Once again the question of unbelievers and of impatient believers, is "Why doesn't God *always* intervene?" "I am willing," said Adolf Hitler to Hermann Rauschning, "to send a million or two million young Germans to their death for my purposes." But when the madman picks up a pen to sign the document, why doesn't God paralyze his hand or strike him dead? When Pius VII excommunicated Napoleon Bonaparte, the great conqueror is alleged to have said, "Does he think that excommunication will make the muskets drop from the hands of my soldiers?" We used to be told when we were boys in school that the muskets did drop. But if a document from the pen of a pope stopped Napoleon, would not a thought in the mind of God stop Hitler? or Stalin? or Mao? So it goes: Why? and Why? and Why?

I have not promised a perfect answer. "Who hath known the mind of the Lord? Or who hath been his counsellor?" the patriarch Job inquires. Certainly this uninspired writer makes no such claim. But I can make a guess. Take it for what it is worth. God does not strike tyrants dead for the same reason that he does not strike you or me dead if we sin or plan a sin. Every mortal sin is outrage to God, but God does not punish the outrage with instant death and hell. "Shall we call down fire from heaven?," said James and John, the "Sons of Thunder." "You know not of what spirit you are," was the reply of the gentle Jesus. If all who displease God were dealt with summarily, the earth would be depopulated. When the sinner opens his mouth to lie or to slander or blaspheme, God does not strike him dumb. When a tempter follows an innocent maiden with lecherous eyes God does not strike him blind and slay him. When Judas went out of the supper room to complete his treacherous plans with the murderers of Jesus, God did not strike him dead at the threshold. It is not God's way. He is a long-suffering God, plenteous in mercy. He wills not the death of the sinner. And He is Almighty: He can produce good out of evil. No man can say how much God can and will endure before He strikes. If He were to strike at all, we should probably think He strikes too often and with too small provocation—especially if He should strike us.

God could indeed prevent even the thought of sin, but only on condition that He take away our free will. Then we should be irresponsible animals or machines in human shape. God seems to think it better that we be free even if freedom is dangerous, than that we should be beasts or mere automata.

Secondly, it is a matter of faith that physical evils are not always calamities. "Be not afraid of them who kill the body," says our Lord, "and after that have no more that they can do." They that die innocently achieve happiness. They achieve it all the more swiftly in proportion to the agony they endure. If they are conscious of their union with Christ as members of His Mystical Body, they may offer their sufferings in union with His, become in effect martyrs and so help in the moral and spiritual progress of the race.

Finally, be it said, this is not defeatism. Ours is not a defeatist religion. We speak much of the Cross. But the Cross is not all. The Divine Victim slain on Calvary did not remain in the grave. His death was not the end. There was the Resurrection. It is our religion that if we suffer with Him we shall be glorified with Him. If that be not sufficient answer to the question, "Why do the innocent suffer?" I am afraid that those of us who see no further will have to wait until the Eternal Light dawns.

Chapter 37

Tell the Truth: Save the World

WHEN Pope Leo XIII opened the Vatican archives to the world, inviting any and all, Catholic, non-Catholic, Jew, agnostic, skeptic, friend or enemy of the Church, to come and make use of that vast treasury of historical documents, with only the stipulation that the guests should present credentials of scholarship, he quoted St. Ambrose who had said fourteen hundred years earlier, "Tell the Truth; God has no need of a lie." The invitation and the quotation were no mere gesture, but a demonstration of courage and honesty. There was in those archives evidence aplenty of the work of the Church as creator and director of Christian civilization; records of trial and triumph; but there was also much first-hand information about scandals amongst the members and the leaders of the Church.

No organization can live for a century, still less for nineteen centuries without harboring an occasional rascal. There is a skeleton in every closet, and it is commonly said that every proud house, if it goes a few generations back, will find a criminal among its forebears. Aristocracy, royalty, nobility stem from usurpers, regicides, murderers, assassins. The first barons were usually robbers; kings came to their thrones generally by killing their predecessors, perhaps their fathers or brothers, and in many cases by a blood-purge of all possible rivals. It would be a rare noble house that would dare lay open its family history to the eyes of the world. But that is what Leo XIII did when he welcomed the world of scholars to the Vatican archives.

The frankest of all historical records are the Sacred Scriptures. They tell the truth, even when the truth is horrifying as in the case of King David's being an adulterer and a murderer; or when it is scandalous, as in the case of St. Peter's swearing that he never knew Jesus Christ. "It must needs be that scandals come," said Jesus; and "A man's enemies will be those of his own household." Before a half century of Christian history had passed, St. Paul had to complain that some Church members were guilty of such vices as were unheard of among the heathen. By the fifth century we find St. Augustine asking and answering in his vivid way: "Who are the enemies of the Church? Pagans? Jews? Worse than these are bad Christians." Always among the great leaders of the Church there is this refreshing truthfulness. Only the lesser and more timorous apologists think it necessary to conceal truth for the sake of edification.

God is affronted with a lie; God is wounded by a lie. If God could be killed He would be murdered by a lie. We do not say that God reveals truth, or teaches truth, or enjoins truth. We say God *is* Truth. Some ancient superstitions maintained that there were two gods, a good god and a bad god, each trying to destroy the other. That was a superstition and a heresy, but what is a superstition or a heresy but the distortion of a truth? Jesus—True God of True God—says, "I am the Truth," and He calls Satan, "Father of lies and of liars."

There, if we can but see it, is the Battle of the Ages, the duel between the Truth and the Lie. We cannot fight the battle for Truth with a lie. Pope St. Pius X in private audience gave to one of our Paulist Fathers, Father Doyle, a motto which that priest quoted incessantly, "We cannot build the Church upon the ruins of charity." Nor, let us add, upon the ruins of Truth. Neither can we build the nation upon the ruins of Truth. There are many traitors and there is much treason in the body politic and in the body ecclesiastic at all times and especially in time of stress and crisis; but the most dangerous traitor is the one who attempts to

serve his country or his Church with a lie; and the most dangerous of all delusions is the idea that a good big thumping lie,
or even a surreptitious lie, can be of use in the defense of Church
or State.

The world of diplomacy, of political maneuvering, the art of
influencing the popular mind, what we have come to call "propaganda"—tragic case of a good word gone wrong—is built upon
the Satanic principle that when a certain end is to be achieved a
lie can be pressed into service of the truth. The Man Who said,
"This is why I have come into the world; to bear witness to the
truth," was surrendered to the mob by the man who said "What
is truth?" Yes, what is truth? says the politician, the diplomat,
the advocate of expediency, the opportunist, the man who considers himself "practical" in contrast to dreamers and idealists and
perfectionists. There is a classic passage on this subject from the
Book of Morals of Pope St. Gregory the Great in the sixth century:

"This simplicity of the just man," he says, "is laughed to scorn.
The wisdom of this world is to hide one's feelings by artifices,
to use language to conceal thought." (Talleyrand, by the way,
sometimes gets credit for that epigram but it was coined twelve
hundred years before him.) "This is the wisdom," continues St.
Gregory, "which makes falsehood seem true and true seem
false . . . This kind of art youth acquires by practice; young men
pay to learn it. But the wisdom of the righteous is contrary to
all this. They seek to avoid deception, to use words to express
their thought, to love the truth because it is the truth and to
avoid falsehood. But again I say this simplicity is made a matter
of derision: the wise of this world believe simplicity to be foolish-
ness and innocent stupidity."

Obviously the world doesn't change. Like the Bourbon kings,
the world forgets nothing and learns nothing. It makes the same
mistakes in the same way forever and forever. The greatest of its
mistakes is to think that good can be gained by the lie.

In 1941, while the second World War was on, General Pershing who had fought in the first World War said, "We can defend all things we hold most dear only if we make up our minds to face the truth without flinching and to act upon the truth without hesitating." On almost the same day the Pope made a fervent appeal for truth-telling in regard to war, and Marshal Pétain was explaining to the French people that their humiliation had been brought about by persistent lying. Neither war would have occurred if presidents, diplomats, directors, statesmen, congresses, parliaments could by some miraculous means have been persuaded to tell the truth.

The first World War ended in 1918. In the 1920's came a flood of books of the "Now It Can Be Told," "More That Must Be Told," "Lying in Wartime" sort. When war is over, truth will out. But when a war is on or is coming on, there are those who hold it is not expedient to tell the truth. But when truth comes out, those who have used the lie, propagated the lie, trusted in the lie, may be in their graves; the evil that they have done lives after them.

A more important objection to the use of the lie is that God is Truth. This is a metaphysical fact. It smacks of the theological. But it is the profoundest truth of all. He who lies, in any cause, crucifies Truth. He who lies does his part in the obliteration of God, one might say in the annihilation of God. If a sufficient number of such persons appear in any land or in the world God cannot but desert the nation or the race. The worst crime against Church or State is treason, a form of lie. But treason to Church or State is in effect treason to Truth. Treason to Truth is treason to God. Church and State are built upon God; and so is all civilization. To save the civilized world the first and most important means is to tell the truth.